P9-ASC-025

Cervantes'
DON QUIXOTE

GREGOR ROY
ASSOCIATE PROFESSOR OF ENGLISH
UNIVERSITY OF GLASGOW

and

RALPH RANALD
ASSISTANT DEAN, LIBERAL ARTS COLLEGE
NEW YORK UNIVERSITY

FINKELSTEIN
MEMORIAL LIBRARY
SPRING VALLEY, N.Y.

004137732

Copyright © 1965 by
Simon & Schuster

All rights reserved. No part of this book
may be reproduced in any form without
permission in writing from the publisher.

Simon & Schuster, Inc.
15 Columbus Circle
New York, NY 10023

Monarch and colophons are trademarks
of Simon & Schuster, registered in the
U.S. Patent and Trademark Office.

ISBN: 0-671-00553-7

Library of Congress Catalog Card Number: 66-1779

Printed in the United States of America

CONTENTS

INTRODUCTION

BIOGRAPHY: CERVANTES' EARLY LIFE: Miguel de Cervantes Saavedra was born in 1547 in Alcala de Henares, near Madrid. He was the fourth son of the seven children of a poverty-stricken physician, who took his family to Madrid in 1561. Cervantes was a student in the city school in 1568, and his teacher, Juan Lopez de Hoyos, seems to have had a considerable influence on the writer's early appreciation of classical literature. In 1569 Cervantes was in Rome, working for a certain Giulio Acquariva, who had spent some time as papal delegate to Spain, We are not certain as to why Cervantes left his native country at this time, for much of his biography is obscure at certain periods. It is probably true, however, that he was fleeing justice, since we know for certain that in September, 1569, the Spanish authorities issued a warrant for the arrest of one "Migual de Cervantes," who had wounded a man in a fight. Defenders of Cervantes have claimed that the name was purely coincidental, but we must remember that this kind of incident was not unusual in those days. The English writer, Christopher Marlowe, was reputedly killed in a tavern brawl, and the Spanish dramatic poet, Lope de Vega, had to leave Spain for a similar reason.

MIDDLE PERIOD: We next hear of Cervantes when, about 1570, he enlisted in a Spanish regiment stationed in Italy. He took part in the famous naval battle of Lepanto on October 7, 1571, and lost the use of his left hand as a result. After a winter in the hospital, he re-entered military service, and fought at Navarino in 1572 and Tunis in 1573. In 1574, when he was returned to Spain, the galley *El Sol* on which he was travelling was captured by Barbary pirates, and Cervantes spent five years in Algiers as a slave. During this period, he made five attempts to escape and indulged in several love intrigues which are often referred to in his works. In 1580 he was released on a ransom of 500 crowns, and was back in Madrid by December of that year. From that time until 1584 we do not know much about his activities, apart from the fact that he was sent by the King

of Spain to Oran on a special mission in 1581, and that in June
of that year he was living in the city of Cartagena. Between
1583 and 1585, however, some of his poems were published
in other men's books. The next event of importance in his life
was his marriage to a lady called Doña Catalina de Palacios
Salazar y Vozmediano, in her village, Esquivias, close to
Madrid. From this point on, his literary career began in earnest.

LATER YEARS: In 1585 his *Galatea* was published, and he
tells us that in the years immediately following this he wrote
twenty to thirty plays, but only two of these early plays are still
extant. In 1587 he was appointed commissary of Andalusia,
during which time he was in continual trouble, being excom-
municated for appropriating grain owned by the Church, and
ending up in jail for illegal seizure of wheat. He spent several
other spells in prison due to disputes with the Treasury Depart-
ment. During this period he wrote the first part of *Don Quixote,*
which went to press in 1604, and was published in Madrid in
January, 1604. At this time he was living in Valladolid, then
the capital, with his family, apparently in sordid and wretched
circumstances. When Madrid became the nation's capital again
in February, 1606, Cervantes probably went to live there. We
know only a few details of his life from this time on: he joined
the Brotherhood of Slaves of the Holy Sacrament in 1609, and
became a member of a literary club called *Academia Selvaje*
in 1612. In 1613 he published the *Novelas Ejemplares,* in 1614
the *Viaje del Parnaso,* and the second part of *Don Quixote*
appeared in 1615. He was stricken with dropsy on April 19,
1616, and wrote the very moving dedication of his *Persiles* to
the Conde de Lemon before dying on April 23, at the age of
sixty-nine. It is an amazing coincidence that William Shakespeare died on the same day.

EDUCATION: We do not know a great deal about Cervantes' formal education. He makes several nostalgic references
to the school in Seville run by the Jesuits, and although he knew
Salamanca, we have no definite evidence that he studied there.
We know for sure, however, that between the years 1568 and
1569 he received a sound humanist education from the scholar,
Juan Lopez de Hoyos. When Queen Isabelle of Valois died,
the scholar and his students wrote a work in her honor, to

which Cervantes contributed a few verses. Apart from this, however, he did not receive much formal education, and he earned the reputation of being a natural, self-instructed genius —or *el ingenio lego,* as his countemporaries called him. He had a keen and inquiring mind, which, coupled with wide reading, gave him a sound knowledge and appreciation of the most influential Italian and Spanish authors, It is certain that he was steeped in the chivalric romances so popular in his day. Yet from the brief account of his life given above, the student can well imagine that the adventures and mishaps of his colorful life, and the people he encountered on his travels, gave him an education in human relationships and attitudes which prevented his becoming pedantic. This intimate knowledge of and sympathy with people show their effect in his major work, *Don Quixote.*

LITERARY CAREER: PLAYS: Drama in Cervantes' day was a very popular art form. About 1585 Cervantes first tried his hand at playwriting, but only two of these early efforts have survived, one called *El Trato de Argel* and the other *La Numancia.* The first of these is totally worthless dramatically, apart from the rather striking depiction of a slave called Saavedra. *La Numancia* contains a few moments of tenderness and power, but is weakly constructed and is of purely historical interest. At the end of his life, in 1615, he published *Eight Comedies and Eight New Interludes,* which vary in type and standard, some being extremely romantic and packed with adventures—like *El Gallardo Español,* for example—and others being more realistic and vividly imaginative—like *Pedro de Urdemalas.* Cervantes seemed to have been more at home with the latter type of theme. On the whole, however, it can be stated that Cervantes was a failure as a playright. He had little or no theatrical sense, and his characters come through as puppets, wooden and badly constructed. Theoretically, he was against theatrical innovation at first, but later changed his mind and encouraged experimentation. Traditionally or experimentally, however, his talents did not lie in drama.

PERSILES AND VIAJE DEL PARNASO: Of these two prose works, *Trabajos de Persiles y Sigismunda* is the more important, but purely for scholarly reasons. It is full of wild, extravagant adventures which take place in ill-defined icy regions, Spain, France, Portugal and Rome. As a novel, it is totally devoid of cohesive theme, plot or characterization. Some critics have tried to defend it artistically by claiming that it was a genuine attempt on Cervantes' part to write a baroque, neo-Byzantine type of experimental work, but even if that is the case, the attempt was a lamentable failure. After the first two books, which are crammed with a plethora of disjointed adventure, the plot completely disappears and the last part of the work consists of some romantic tales containing a few side comments on contemporary mores. The amazing fact is that Cervantes considered it his greatest book, and the work which would earn him immortality. Even in the dedication to the second part of *Don Quixote,* Cervantes says of *Persiles,* "It will be either the worst book or the best, that was ever written in our language . . . and I repent of having said the worst, for my friends assure me it will attain the limit of possible goodness." *Viaje del Parnaso* is a tediously allegorical book commenting on the works of a hundred and fifty poets, but it is of interest only when Cervantes forgets the unnatural pomposity of the style and lapses—on very rare occasions—into his own language and mode of address. It was modeled on an Italian work called *Viaggio in Parnaso,* 1589.

NOVELAS EJEMPLARES: These *"Exemplary Tales"* were published in 1613. The title alone is worthy of a brief comment. The word *"novela"* was an innovation in Spanish, and meant a short artistically handled tale, not a full-length novel, written in the style of the Italian *"novella."* Cervantes added the adjective "exemplary" to the title of his collection to prevent their contents being associated with the indecencies of their Italian counterparts, since he intended his work to be read by a "respectable" audience. Despite this, some of them are pretty gross and scabrous, particularly one entitled *El Casamiento Engañoso,* but the reader must consider the tastes of the age in which the collection was published. His *"novelas"* cover quite a wide range, however, from the credible realism of *Rinconete y Cortodillo* to the picaresque romanticism of *El Celoso Extremeño.* There is also a stylistic fluidity and charm of plot in many of these tales, which gives the impression that Cervantes actually enjoyed writing them. He claimed that his *"novelas"* were completely original: "They are my own, neither imitated, nor stolen; my wit begot them, my pen bore them." While this boast is not completely accurate—*El Celoso Extremeño* is taken from an episode recounted by the Italian epic poet, Boiardo, for example—the *"novelas"* are on the whole fresh, imaginative, and interesting.

DON QUIXOTE: Since Part I of *El Ingenioso Hidalgo Don Quixote de la Mancha,* commonly known as *Don Quixote,* was completed in 1603 or 1604, the work was probably at least conceived when Cervantes was in jail. Part I was very successful, going into ten editions by 1615. By that same year Cervantes had also completed Part II, which had been dragging on in composition for some time. It is possible that the author started *Don Quixote* as a *"novela,"* making it merely the description of a crazy character which would amuse his readers. Once he had started it, however, many literary forces came into play: parody and satire were becoming popular; picaresque novels were growing in number; and pastorals were going out of fashion. Furthermore, Cervantes undoubtedly grasped the importance of the romantic, chivalric aspects of the work once he had started it. Although the chivalric age was past, its spirit lived on in many literary forms, and the student must recognize this fact in taking into consideration the satirical aspects of *Don Quixote.* Some critics have tried to read into Cervantes' work the influence of such Italian writers as Boiardo, Pulci, and Ariosto, or of other Spanish novels such at *Tirant lo Blanch* or *El Caballero Cifar.* There are similarities, but *Don Quixote* can be safely regarded as a thoroughly original work.

AVELLANEDA'S DON QUIXOTE: After the great success of Part I of *Don Quixote,* a second part was published in 1614 by someone who called himself Alonso Fernandez de Avellaneda. During the Renaissance, of course, writing sequels to other people's books was quite common—Ariosto, for example, did this to Boiardo. The preface to Avellaneda's Part II, however, caused Cervantes some hurt, since it was particularly insulting in nature. This prompted Cervantes to change the direction of his own Part II—quite literally so, since he decided that Don Quixote would now go to Barcelona rather than Saragossa. If nothing else, Avellaneda spurred Cervantes on to complete the

final part of his work, which had been going on at a desultory
pace for some time. In the last chapters of *Don Quixote*, Cervantes even makes some veiled but amusing references to the
false Part II, and the abusive preface to Avellaneda's work was
answered in Cervantes' own prologue, without descending to
any cheap level of retaliation. Scholars have worked at some
length to find the true identity of Avellaneda, which was apparently a pseudonym, but with no success. The existence of the
"pseudo-Quixote" is in fact relatively unimportant, apart from
the fact that Part I was considered important enough to continue, and that it prompted Cervantes to finish it.

**LITERARY BACKGROUND OF THE AGE: THE RENAISSANCE
AND HUMANISM:**   The period at the end of the Middle
Ages known as the Renaissance was a time not only in which
the classics of antiquity were unearthed and examined, but also
in which men looked forward to new cultural and exploratory
ventures. There was a spirit abroad of rebellion against sub-
mission to theological dogma and intellectual stagnation which
had tended to stifle individuality of expression in the arts.
Although the Renaissance really flourished in the 16th Century,
its genesis can be traced back to the 14th Century, when
Petrarch set the tone for what we may loosely term "modern
thinking." The fall of Constantinople to the Turks in 1453 is
often cited as the real beginning of the Renaissance, because of
the flood of Greek scholars who sought refuge in Italy, bringing
with them a vast store of classical knowledge, which they im-
parted to an eager audience. It should be remembered, however, that Greek culture had taken root outside the Byzantine
Empire long before 1453. Nevertheless, the 15th Century was
indeed the time when the intellectual excitement of the Renaissance was felt at its highest pitch. Interest in Latin was resusci-
tated, Plato was studied as well as Aristotle, the science of
philology opened up new doors to the study of classical
language, and science embarked on new voyages which still
have their impact. The term "humanism" is applied to the
Renaissance attitude whereby the individual was celebrated
more than ever before, and scholarship served humanity. It was
the age of inventions—gunpowder, and the mariner's compass,
for example—and the age in which printing revolutionized the
dissemination of knowledge. The fine arts—music, sculpture,

painting and architecture—took new life, and literature looked to the ancient classical texts as its model. Criticism as an art form in itself flourished, basing its premises on Aristotelian doctrine. And throughout the whole movement, Europe looked to Italy as the core of Renaissance civilization. The student must not get the impression, however, that this cultural outburst led to universal, aesthetic bliss. In certain cases, it resulted in unbridled lawlessness and bouts of pagan licentiousness. In literature monstrous tomes of stuffy, neo-classical pedantry were produced, and an over-accentuation on the cult of the individual led to a great deal of intellectual and artistic chaos. This was understandable however, in view of the stifling atmosphere which had permeated Europe throughout the feudalism of the Middle Ages. Historically it was a period of fervor and optimism; culturally it was a time of flourishing activity; intellectually it was an age of hope.

CERVANTES AND THE SPANISH RENAISSANCE: GENERAL COMMENTS: The 16th Century is known as *El Siglo de Oro,* the Golden Age, of Spanish history, in which Spain rose in power under the Emperor Charles V and was influenced by three great movements—the Reformation, the Counter-Reformation, and the Renaissance. By the end of the 16th Century, an economic and cultural decline began to set in, although the arts still flourished in what was called the "baroque" style. Some critics have claimed that the baroque was a direct outgrowth of the Counter-Reformation. But that cannot be entirely true, since the Counter-Reformation was well under way by the end of the Council of Trent in 1563, and baroque did not appear to any great extent before 1600. Under Philip II, Spanish literature found its sources in the Spanish Reformation, the intellectual tone of which was set by Erasmus and Northern European humanists. It is true that most of Erasmus' works were put on the Index in 1559. But by that time, humanism, or, if we want to be more precise, Erasmism, has influenced the thinking of Spanish artists, writers, and intellectuals. In this respect the Spanish Renaissance was unique, inasmuch as it received a cultural impact from Italy, and was also hammered into its unique shape by the twin intellectual blows of the Reformation and Counter-Reformation.

RENAISSANCE ATMOSPHERE: Cervantes was born when the Spanish Renaissance was at its peak. The Spanish Empire was in the flull glow of triumph, and universities, cathedrals and palaces were springing up as wealth poured in from Peru, Mexico and the East. In the arts, sculpture, poetry and music flourished, and the instincts of artisans were expressed architecturally and culturally in works of intricate beauty and exquisite richness. Artists and scholars poured into Spain, and Cervantes himself once said that everyone in France could speak Spanish. Among the aristocracy, there was an increasing interest in the arts, and universities intensified their classical curricula. In view of what we have said before about the Renaissance in general, it is interesting to note the way in which the cultural hunger of Europe was satisfied by a process of growth and interchange. Spain was particularly interesting, since it was the recipient and the donor of such variegated influences as the Moorish, Oriental, Italian, and Northern European. Add to this, passionate, proud, chivalric and mystical qualities which are ingrained in the Spanish character, and we have a good idea of the heritage which influenced Cervantes in the writing of his masterpiece *Don Quixote.*

THE INQUISITION: One of the retrogressive and repressive influences during the Spanish Renaissance was the spiritual-cum-temporal movement known as the Inquisition. It is interesting to note that while ecclesiastical reaction against the free-thinking aspects of the Renaissance in Italy came at the end of the cultural upsurge, in Spain it was a contemporary movement. There are very complex reasons for this, and historians and theologians of all denominations have written voluminously on the whole question of the extreme orthodoxy which coexisted at this time with a spirit of intellectual inquiry. One effect on the Spanish literature of the period is very obvious: on the whole it is much less uninhibitedly obscene than much of what was being written elsewhere.

PATRONAGE: Spain was different from the rest of Renaissance Europe in its attitude to patronage. In Italy, it had become almost modish for royalty and aristocracy to sponsor the arts. In France, Francis I was lavish in his generosity to cultural ventures. The tone of the Spanish attitude, however, was set by Isabella, who gave a modicum of support to the arts so long as they did not offend her narrow standards. It has been suggested that had she taken a more liberal attitude toward patronage, her successors and the aristocracy would have followed suite, and the Spanish Renaissance would have risen to even greater heights. This is an unconvincing argument. Patronage had many restrictive drawbacks, and Spanish Renaissance literature has democratic elements lacking in that of others.

PRINTING: In 1474 the first book in Spain was printed, and we know that there was a press in Barcelona in 1475. By the end of the 15th Century, most Spanish provincial towns had their own printing press, usually operated by Germans. The intellectual and sociological effects of this were tremendous, of course. Apart from religious works, the presses produced classics, as well as the romantic literature so fashionable at that time. Libraries began to spring up, ideas were interchanged, and a deeper knowledge of Spanish and European literature lent a rich academic tone to the Spanish world into which Cervantes was born.

CULTURAL INFLUENCES: Cervantes lived in an age of cultural, literary and intellectual giants, all of whom left their mark on the times, and some of whom had a direct effect on Cervantes. Erasmus, for example, had a tremendous humanistic influence throughout Europe; Rabelais had written *Pantagruel* and *Gargantua;* Ariosto's *Orlando Furioso* had an enormous influence on Cervantes; El Greco, the great painter, was born the same year as Cervantes; the great mythical poet, St. John of the Cross, and the world's greatest dramatist, Shakespeare, were contemporaries. These few names alone should give the student some idea of the cultural climate in which Cervantes wrote *Don Quixote,* We must remember, too, that education was not restricted to the wealthy, and many poor children found their way to one or another of Spain's great universities, where they achieved eminence. There was a genuine spirit of adventure abroad—the few details we have of Cervantes' life bear witness to that—and an expansive mood of creativity permeated the Spanish atmosphere. We should bear all this in mind when we read of the mission of the strange knight-errant, and of his peasant who hoped to govern an island.

CERVANTES AND THE COUNTER-REFORMATION: This was also the age in which there was a general upsurge of interest in religion, with heresies arising in Northern Europe which continually threatened the Catholic orthodoxy of Spain. When Cervantes was born, the Council of Trent was taking place, and when he was growing up, the Counter-Reformation was in full swing. Some historians have drawn a gloomy picture of the Spanish Renaissance as being continually under the eyes of the Inquisition. Yet Cervantes, Lope de Vega, Velázquez, and El Greco were not prevented from producing masterpieces, and the main complaint Cervantes seems to have had against the Counter-Reformation was that it banned dueling. It should be pointed out, however, that there are allegorical interpretations of *Don Quixote* which point to the fact that he was at times being highly critical of ecclesiastical authoritarianism. Taken at its face value alone, however, the book does not give signs of having been written in an atmosphere of stringent censorship. It gives, in fact, a wonderfully colorful portrait of the sweeping grandeur of Spain, its landscapes, its people, and its spaciousness. Throughout it all, too, there is the spirit of healthy laughter in *Don Quixote,* and a notable absence of gloom.

CERVANTES AND THE AGE: Apart from the more universal aspects of *Don Quixote,* which we will be discussing later in detail, it is a work which shows Cervantes to have been what Havelock Ellis called "the most typical of Spaniards." Cervantes draws us into the 16th-Century Spain with masterly strokes: the reader drinks wine with the goatherds of the Sierra Morena; he shares the bacon and eggs in Sancho's poverty-stricken home. The Spanish character of the day is brought to the foreground of our imagination with vivid intensity. We are examining Cervantes here on one level, of course—that of the genial Castilian, the loyal Spaniard. He talks of Spain as being "the center of foreigners and the mother of the nations." In *La Galatea,* for example, he claims that "our age is more fortunate than that of the Greeks and Romans." Surveying the whole of the 16th Century, Cervantes says that during the reigns of

Charles V and Philip II, Spain lived in a "golden age." The student should not get the impression from all this that the author of *Don Quixote* was totally unaware of the evils of the times. Every great writer in every age has deplored the crass features of his era. In Cervantes' works, therefore, we find such phrases as "the age of iron," and he continually denounces the depravities and tyrannies which beset the times. Nor does he let his fellow countrymen off the hook so easily. It might be worthwhile commenting on some of the detailed criticisms which Cervantes made of his age. This might help to explain many facets of life exposed to *Don Quixote*.

CERVANTES AS CRITIC OF THE AGE: It could be said that Cervantes' main attack was on the shallowness of his age, and he was highly critical of external display in contrast with inner integrity. There was an atmosphere of restless discontent abroad which he found unhealthy. Beggars, robbers and vagrants swarmed the streets, while there was a marked difference between the wealthy comfort of nobles and priests, and the abject living conditions of the poor. Cervantes believed in self improvement, but not at the expense of others, and the student should bear this in mind when he comes to compare Don Quixote, who wished to improve mankind, with Sancho Panza, who desired self-aggrandizement. Cervantes was therefore rebellious against the injustices of the age, but was nevertheless conventional in his belief in proportional social equality. It was undoubtedly fortunate that Cervantes led the life he did, for otherwise he might well have missed the opportunity of consorting with beggars, thieves, galley-slaves and gypsies. He was a child of the Renaissance, inasmuch as he had a healthy cultural appetite and an intellectually greedy mind. Yet *Don Quixote* abounds with a sense of sympathy for humanity which might not have been there had he been reared in an entirely pedantic atmosphere. He might then have given us a weighty tome groaning with Renaissance pedantry.

RENAISSANCE INFLUENCES ON CERVANTES: Cervantes adhered, on the whole, to the literary conventions of the Renaissance in such matters as dramatic unities, while on the other hand he scorned the useless display of knowledge which filled many contemporary humanist works. During his five years in Italy, he imbued a great deal of Renaissance culture and knew Italian well enough to read Tasso and Ariosto in the original. He makes reference to Dante and Petrarch, and, as we have seen, was influenced by the Italian art form, the *"novella."* Of his own Spanish contemporaries, he particularly admired the works of Luis de Leon and Velez de Guevara. But Cervantes was a typical Renaissance figure in the uniquely Spanish Renaissance way, whereby the new flowering of classical knowledge took place within the context of medieval influences. Cerventes did not withdraw into the past and express himself in entirely neo-classical terms. He drew on the classical and medieval past, and mingled the aesthetic with the moral. And in *Don Quixote,* all these elements are expressed in the terms of the present. His work is an admixture of all these trends: classical, medieval, aesthetic and ethical, with the result that, artistically, *Don Quixote* is a work pointing to the future.

CERVANTES AND LANGUAGE:　　In the Spanish Renaissance, there was a growing humanist cult of using the vernacular, with its ballads and proverbs, in various types of writings. Cervantes fell heir to this spirit, and although he delighted in the beauties of Greek, Latin, and Italian, he loved his native tongue with its rich idioms and popular phraseology. As he himself said, "Homer wrote in Greek and Virgil in Latin. The German, Spaniard, or Basque should each use his own language." In many ways *Don Quixote* was an adequate response to a plea by the writer, Luis de León, that books should be written in Castilian so that ordinary people could read them. The language of the book combines those rare qualities of subtle nuances and substantial realities which are distinctive features of the Castilian language. And when we consider some other conflicting themes of the novel—reality and unreality, truth and fantasy, the commonplace and the dream world—it can be seen how appropriate the language is to the theme. Cervantes was fascinated by language, particularly that of the people, and studied the dialects of Biscay, the Basque, Portugal, and Valencia. This interest—typical of Spanish Renaissance humanism—combined with his eye for detail and innate powers of psychological perception, gave him an uncommon background for the writing of his novel. All these influences have a bearing on the tone, style, and atmosphere of his novel.

CERVANTES AND CASTILE: The art and literature of Castile has a rich and deep heritage. It produced the lyricism of Luis de León, the mystical poems of St. John of the Cross, together with a mass of epics, romances and plays. In art, Castilian sensibility is powerfully expressed in the fusion of massive substance and delicacy of Veláquez' paintings, and in literature it is best exemplified in Cervantes' *Don Quixote,* particularly in the characters of the knight and his page. This sensibility took the form of a combination of the bizarre and the subtle, exuberance and refinement, the spirit and the flesh. And throughout it all runs a rare spirit of stoical endurance and solidity of character. If we look for all these qualities in *Don Quixote,* we will find them. Sancho, for example, who is drawn at one stage as a matter-of-fact, sensible type, is at times pulled into the world of fantasy and even becomes mellow as the governor of Barataria. Don Quixote himself embraces all the qualities of the Castilian heritage: he is a massively drawn figure, restlessly energetic, with amazing powers of endurance. Add to all this an intensity of character and a touch of subtle irony, and we have a synthesis of the unique genius of Castile. And its greatest literary ambassador is, without a doubt, Cervantes.

CERVANTES, THE MIDDLE AGES, AND THE RENAISSANCE: Another aspect of Cervantes' uniquely Spanish Renaissance temperament was his midway position between the Western sense of inquiry and an Oriental sense of fatalism. He is modern in that he stands on a permanent bridge constructed of all the best medieval and Renaissance elements. The contemporary spirit of external searching was tempered by his deep-rooted sense of medieval spirituality. An interesting comparison has been made between Cervantes and Christopher Columbus, based on an observation of the Spanish critic, Salvador de Madariaga, that the man who discovered the New World had a medieval mind. Cervantes was medieval in his belief in absolute values and in man's dependence on a power higher than himself. Yet we must not believe that this resulted in a static intellectual or artistic position. It is almost as if Cervantes

allowed his deep-rooted and rich medieval heritage to be
re-fashioned in Renaissance terms. Thus his spirit, his intellect,
and his artistry were in a continual state of movement prompted
by the restless energy of his age. When he was in Africa in
1579, for example, he wrote a letter in which he said that his
imagination was in constant turmoil. While sharing the Medieval
and Renaissance belief in the primacy of the soul, he also knew
its torments through bitter personal experience. He was highly
sensitive and thoroughly honest artistically—for example, in
Persiles he admits his own fears as a soldier. Yet again his
sensitivity, and particularly his sense of aesthetic values, was
thoroughly Renaissance in its vigor while completely Medieval
in its depths. Here again Cervantes was very typical of the
Spanish Renaissance in that his attitude represents the ultimate
fulfillment of medieval values rather than a break from them.
In his *Galatea,* he speaks of his appreciation of beauty in
architecture and painting, and says that he was particularly
interested in the various shades of coloring in the portraits he
knew. However, the student must not glibly describe Cervantes
as being simply a "child of the Renaissance." To begin with,
he was part of the *Spanish* Renaissance, which had unique
aspects to it. Furthermore, Cervantes owed a great spiritual,
intellectual, and aesthetic debt to the Middle Ages, and this is
worth remembering when *Don Quixote* is under consideration.
As we shall see, this work can be viewed from many angles.
But no matter how we view it, we must be aware of Cervantes'
position regarding Medievalism, and the Renaissance, and of
the influence of both cultures on his art.

CERVANTES AND HIS PHILOSOPHY OF AESTHETICS:
There has been some dispute over Cervantes' idea of beauty.
He loved Nature, particularly when embellished by man, and
this was typical of the Italian Renaissance. He called this "a
third Nature to which I can give no name." His sense of color
seems to have been sharpened with the years, for his later
works abound in the warmth of color. He was overwhelmed
by the artistic effect of the Renaissance on such cities as Toledo,
Seville, Milan, and particularly Naples, which he called "the
best city of Europe and of the whole world." Critics have attacked Cervantes' philosophy of aesthetics on two counts. First,
they say that Don Quixote and Sancho Panza by no means

depict beauty in any form. This is easily answered: they were not meant to be "beautiful" characters, and, furthermore, Cervantes rebelled in a way against the Renaissance insistence on perfect outer form. He looked more for inner qualities. Secondly, they say that his philosophy of beauty was superficial and based on the Renaissance theory of imitation. To answer this, one has to understand that Cervantes imitated only as part of his continual probing and searching for real, eternal aesthetic values which he could use as a base to offset the fluctuating, presumptuous and vulgar taste of the people he called the *vulgo*.

CERVANTES, HUMANISM, AND HUMANITY: At this point it would be well to clarify the meaning of *vulgo*. Perhaps the best definition is given by Cervantes himself in *Don Quixote,* where he says, "And do not think by the *vulgo* I mean only humble folk or people, for the ignorant, be he lord or prince, must be included in the term." Cervantes always had a great respect for the individual, but was suspicious of the masses. This led to his having a two-sided attitude to people, which affected his views as a Spanish Renaissance humanist. As we have seen, he loved the language, proverbs and ballads of the people, yet he deplored the vulgarity of taste which seems to go along with mass thinking. (As a side comment, the student might be interested to note that when this criticism is made today, it is not new.) It should again be pointed out, however, that this suspicion was not directed merely at the lower classes, and Cervantes was well aware that insipid values and crassness can exist as well among the aristocracy. We will see, for example, how his depiction of the upper classes in *Don Quixote* is more vague and shadowy than that of the lower classes. The Duke and Duchess, for example, are completely outshadowed as characters by the Don and his squire. Even his most wretched characters have some endearing qualities: when Sancho is in dire need, Maritornes very kindly gives him a glass of wine, for example, and throughout the novel there is a sense of compassion for the poor. It is interesting to note that this bold, realistic description of lower class characters is linked with Cervantes' humanistic views on the Spanish Renaissance. For in Spain the spirit of flourishing literary endeavor was in constant danger of being atrophied by a tortured style, just as in France it eventually was stifled by wit and in Italy by a rarified exclusiveness. Cervantes resisted all this in his writing of *Don Quixote*. He hated the thought of paying fealty to an élite literary cult or clique—known in Spanish as *culteranismo*. Generally speaking, therefore, it can be safely said that Cervantes learned from the best aspects of Renaissance humanism, but rebelled against its more stultifying features. Regarding humanity, he had a great sense of and respect for the human spirit, coupled with a genuine sympathy for the foibles of mankind. On the other hand, this was tempered by a respect for conventional social stratafication, while he deplored vulgarity of taste, and crassness of sensitivity irrespective of class lines.

TWO FICTIONAL FORMS WHICH AFFECTED CERVANTES' DON QUIXOTE

1. THE ROMANCES OF CHIVALRY: GENERAL COMMENTS: This literary genre, which Cervantes was in some respects ridiculing in *Don Quixote,* had many ludicrous aspects. The romances had fairy tale plots, the inevitable victory of knights over apparently insurmountable odds, all couched in overblown, florid prose, The modern reader would find them boring, ridiculous, and puerile, but they made delightful reading for the literate public of the late Middle Ages and early Renaissance. Yet we must not be too disparaging of them as an art form. They were, after all, the first real ventures in novel writing. Furthermore, they *did* extol some rather admirable virtues, such as bravery, fair play, loyalty in love, and a general sense of honor. It is often modish, of course, to scorn these qualities, and it must be admitted that they were lauded in an absurdly exaggerated way in these romances. Yet these qualities are still preferable to cruelty, brutishness of manners, and dishonesty in human relationships. It is very important that the student remember both aspects of these romances when he comes to appraise *Don Quixote*. For there is a very good case to be made for claiming that Cervantes was at one ridiculing the romances as such, with their overabundance of medievalisms, and praising the virtues for which they—and he—stood.

THE SENTIMENTAL NOVELS: These had a wide following in Cervantes' day. They told of unhappy lovers and their attempts—often futile—at finding a solution to their dilemma. The most famous of these in Spanish literature was called *Selva de Adventuras,* by Jeronimo de Contreras. Some of these sentimental tales were in epistle form, like *Lucindaro y Medusina,* by Juan de Segura. Cervantes drew on this tradition in some of the tales which he incorporated into the framework of *Don Quixote.*

THE PASTORAL NOVELS: Pastoral novels, with their idyllic settings, unreal backgrounds, and sighing, languishing shepherds, first made their appearance on the literary scene as the literature of romantic chivalry began to decline. The most famous of these was the *Diana* of *Jorge de Montemayor,* which, with its simple plot, mingling of prose and verse, absence of sincere or deep emotions, and magical elements, set the whole tone of all later Spanish pastorals. Again, their influence is seen in *Don Quixote.*

THE MOORISH NOVELS: These were romances which for a time had a unique vogue, the best of which is the *Historia del Abencerraje y la hermosa Xarifa,* which was first incorporated into *Diana* as a short novel, and republished independently in 1565. Unlike the other romances, this type has a sincerity of tone and a straightforward narrative style, and contains a considerable amount of charm. These Moorish tales are not unlike the *"novelas"* which Cervantes wrote so effectively.

2. THE PICARESQUE NOVEL: GENERAL COMMENTS: This is a type of realistic fiction which has been described as the "romance of roguery" and which became popular in the 16th and 17th Centuries. Spain set the tone for the picaresque form, which was not confined to novels, but found its way into poems, plays, and memoirs. It is usually connected with the novel, however. A picaresque novel is really one in which criminal life is described realistically, with the condition that the rogue is the central figure and not just an incidental character. In Spanish picaresque novels, the criminal usually works for several masters, whose trades are often lampooned. They are humorous satires, though often hard and cynical in tone, and are usually directed against the idealism of popular fiction.

For example, the criminal's family tree is often outlined, ridiculing the aristocracy. While picaresque novels rejoice in and even celebrate the life of the underworld, they do so in a tone of protest against the life of bourgeois and aristocratic respectability. The picaresque novels are also a critical commentary on the economic and social conditions of contemporary Spain, which were precarious. Beggars, thieves and vagabonds roamed the streets, and there was a prevailing atmosphere of sloth and decadence, the aftermath of centuries of power and glory.

LAZARILLO DE TORMES: This is the most famous of the picaresque novels, and was published in 1554. The author is unknown, but we can infer from its contents that he must have been a man of little education but keen intelligence and perception, who was highly critical of the abuses of church and state. He seems to have come under the influence of Erasmus, and had an intense desire to reform society, particularly the church, from within. The final version suggests that some censorship had taken place before publication.

CHARACTERS AND PLOT: The novel is in seven parts, or *trataros*. The criminal's family descent is given by way of parodying the aristocracy. Lazarillo, the "hero", then works for a blind man and a priest, and here it is evident that hunger is meant to justify rascality. The third *trataro* is the most important, for it is here that the Spanish nation is satirized for its vainglorious posture, mismanagement, and parasitic attitudes. The fifth *trataro* is interesting, showing Lazarillo working for a Church indulgence-seller. The "hero" ironically ends up happy and prosperous.

WHY LAZARILLO IS IMPORTANT: This short work was tremendously popular. There are many reasons for its importance: it is told briefly; it is written in the first person, which was an innovation; its types were easily defined; and it was utterly honest and sincere. This short book did a great deal to raise the whole tone of the realistic novel, and pointed the way to more important works of this nature. In particular, it should be remembered as one of the great, influential forerunners of *Don Quixote*.

FOUR MAJOR ASPECTS OF CERVANTES AS PHILOSOPHER AND INTELLECTUAL

1. CERVANTES AND THE EPIC TRADITION: The great historical deeds accomplished by Spain in the 16th Century seem to suggest that some great epic themes would arise. Truth had grown to epic proportions, and history itself could be written in this style—as in Sir Walter Raleigh's *History of the World*. Yet outside the realm of historical reality, there was an overwhelming desire on the part of lyric poets to write epics with purely imaginative themes. Cervantes himself once objected that churchmen who wrote poetry seemed particularly unwilling to admit it. In 1572 *Os, Lusiades,* a historical epic by Camoés, was published, and its claim to depict true history brought to light an argument concerning historical and fictional truth. In his *Persiles,* Cervantes expresses some very strong views on the subject. Claiming that a historian has a choice, he says that truth nevertheless has a magic of its own and must be recorded, even if it does not *seem* to be the truth. Cervantes goes on to claim that some things which do not supersede truth nevertheless defy man's imagination, and are therefore worthy of epic writing. The story of King Arthur is a good example: Cervantes would accept this as worthy of an epic despite its myth, and Milton would reject it because of its myth.

Cervantes also believed in the necessity of idealizing epic themes and heroes, as did Virgil and Homer, and his complaint about many Renaissance epics was that they lacked vividness, idealism, and universality. Recalling our comments about the differences between the Italian and Spanish Renaissance movements, we should point out that there were also differences between Spanish and non-Spanish epics. In Spanish epics there is an intertwining of the real and the unreal, a blending of myth and fact, a mingling of truth and fantasy. This is very important in any consideration of *Don Quixote*. There is one scene in the book, for example, when the inn-keeper reads in a history book that Diego Garcia de Paredes had halted an army single-handedly, and he believes it. By believing this, and thus changing the imaginary into the real, he became the portrait of a typically Spanish trait. In *Don Quixote*, Cervantes overcame this danger by raising the commonplace to epic significance. All Don Quixote's most fantastic happenings, for example, are given a natural setting, and the supernatural effects of the novel take place in a narrow space, heightening the characterization and giving the events epic proportions.

Cervantes believed in blending the worlds of imagination and truth, and in the sonnet which prefaces his *Novelas Ejemplares,* he tells us that his tales are but a setting for the "jewel of truth." Yet in writing *Don Quixote,* which is really an epic in prose, Cervantes must have faced great personal difficulties, since he had an inordinate passion for the absolute truth of history. In an interesting passage in *Persiles* he tells us how he approached such a problem. By extending the boundaries of what is commonly called "history," the writer can sing of humble things by magnifying them to epic proportions through giving free rein to his imagination. His epic thesis in *Don Quixote* was in fact to make the impossible believable while operating in a real world inhabited by real people. Furthermore, he outdid the classical epic writers in at least one respect: while they wrote in a half-real world of myth and divinity, Cervantes wrote of his own times and people, elevating them to heights of glory while sustaining a mixed atmosphere of fantasy and reality. Note, for example, that when Don Quixote leaves his books, he does not simply walk out of the real world into a world of fantasy. He in fact walks into a more fantastic world of reality, and becomes more real at every turn in this new dimension.

One comment should be made here regarding Cervantes' attitude to the epic in the light of his position in the Spanish Renaissance. As we have seen, he rebelled against certain aspects of it while adhering to others. One of Cervantes' objections to contemporary romances and plays was that they obeyed no classical regulations, and in this respect he was a thoroughgoing traditionalist. An epic cannot succeed, he claimed, without obedience to the spirit of time-honored laws. Characters would be incredible and incidents unconvincing. In *Don Quixote,* he obeyed the epic spirit, and succeeded in giving us the most credibly incredible character in fiction.

√2. CERVANTES, RELIGION AND HUMANITY: *Don Quixote* has been described as a "bible of humanity," and while this is

true in one sense, it opens up many questions regarding Cervantes' attitude to religion and humanity. To begin with, he lived in a century and a country which produced the devout lyrics of Luis de León and the mystical verse of St. John of the Cross. But this age also produced the Counter-Reformation and the Inquisition. What was Cervantes' attitude, then, to religion and the Church? His feelings for humanity are demonstrated by the very fact that he spoke out vehemently against capital punishment. His declaration that bravery and cruelty are incompatible goes hand in hand with his belief that courageous satire should not be confused with contemptuous jibes at other men. In *Don Quixote,* for example, he suggests that animals can teach men a lesson in friendly cohabitation, and there are passages in which compassion is shown toward the maimed, the aged, and the poor. Note that at one point Sancho is warned against speaking harshly to his wife. Cervantes' attitude to marriage is generous for a 16th Century Spaniard, since he repeats his belief that marriage should be entered on the desire and choice of the parties concerned. His satire, too, is always tempered with justice, and while he may denounce the hypocrisies and inadequacies of certain friars, ministers of justice, and doctors, he is always careful to point out that there *are* many people in the Church, law, and the medical profession who are absolutely sincere and competent. In this respect he is very like Geoffrey Chaucer.

This brings us to the question of the inter-relation of morality and formal religion in Cervantes' personal philosophy. From what we have just seen, it would appear that Cervantes placed man and his private ethical standards above ritualized religion —the insubordinate renegade in *Don Quixote,* for example, is described as "morally an honest man." On the other hand, he tells us in his *Persiles* that God is everywhere, and from *Don Quixote* we get his opinion that God's will dominates everything. In *Don Quixote,* too, continual professions of the Catholic faith are made, and of the "Church which I adore as a faithful Catholic and Christian." Critics have interpreted these pronouncements in two ways. The first and obvious one was that he was utterly sincere in what he said, and that he believed whole-heartedly in the dogma and ritual of the Roman Church. The second interpretation is that Cervantes overdoes his role as a Catholic apologist, that he reiterated his professions of faith to prevent his being censured by the Inquisition, and that he can therefore be charged with hypocrisy.

Both of these arguments can be defended easily by the two schools of thought. The truth of the matter, however, is probably that Cervantes was indeed a practising Catholic, but an extremely enlightened one who believed that the eternal truths of Christianity demand the freedom of the individual conscience. ✓ He was certainly writing as a Catholic, and was criticising many aspects of the ecclesiastical structure from within its framework. Some critics have pointed to the irreverence of such incidents as Don Quixote's making a rosary out of his shirt-tail, for example, and have inferred from this a concomitant irreligious attitude on Cervantes' part, It could be argued, however, that this is a kind of satirical criticism of religious rituals born of Cervantes' familiarity with them, and that it in no way implies that he disbelieved the virtues which these rituals represent.

We also must not forget that there was a deep-rooted mysticism in Cervantes which often goes unappreciated. He believed that there is a harmony of Nature, that it is man's sacred duty to live in harmony with Nature, and that Nature is, by its very creation, submissive to the will of God. His argument against capital punishment, for example, is centered on his statement that "God will punish." Cervantes openly declared that man is salvaged or condemned according to the intention behind his deeds, and in taking this position he is saying in fact that man's soul is engaged in a perpetual dialogue with God alone. Cervantes did not deplore the external, tangible symbols of religion which are so important to the Spanish Catholic mind. What he did deplore, however, was the abuse of these symbols, particularly when such abuse impinged on the freedom and dignity of the individual. His was truly a religion of humanity.

3. CERVANTES AND REALITY: From one viewpoint, *Don Quixote* is a book which probes the nature of reality. Cervantes, with his inquiring mind and love of truth, was deeply involved in this problem. He lived in an age in which the opinions of men were being distrubed by such questions, and when the rigid answers of Scholastic Philosophy were being put to the test everywhere. In one way, therefore, Don Quixote's exploits constitute Cervantes' way of putting appearance to the test. His mission can be seen as one of continual experimentation, a process of seeking proofs and having counterproofs flung back at him when he is rebuffed. We are in fact told, "One must actually touch appearances with one's hand if one is not to be deceived." We learn that reality can be distorted in many ways and under many guises. When Sancho sees sheep and windmills, for example, Don Quixote sees knights and giants. But Cervantes is not just lauding Sancho and mocking the Don for their respective viewpoints. To the strange knight-errant, the sheep and the windmills really *are* knights and giants. Cervantes, in his examination of reality, finds that external appearance is deceptive, and this discrepancy between the real and the unreal is tested by the very characters of Sancho and the Don. The knight's delusion is delusion only to Sancho, and furthermore, as the characters develop we note how Sancho himself becomes a victim of enchantment, and the knight then becomes more real than his squire. In the character of Don Quixote, Cervantes is in fact making an inquiry into the philosophy whereby nothing really exists but a world of dreams from which man may possibly awake into a more complete reality. When a kitchen wench becomes a princess in Don Quixote's eyes, Cervantes is translating reality onto a higher plateau and exposing it to the light of philosophic scrutiny. Don Quixote's outer senses may be deceived, but his inner conviction is undaunted. And it was this inner conviction which was of paramount importance to Cervantes as a man. By its very existence and survival, it seemed a testimony to Cervantes of man's basic worth.

4. CERVANTES AND HUMOR: Much has been written about the theory of humor, in an attempt to explain why people laugh at certain things at particular times under unique circumstances. Yet it remains for the most part one of the mysteries of life. It is interesting that 16th-Century Spain, for all its medieval mysticism, its soul-searching character, and its Inquisition, produced in Cervantes one of the world's greatest humorists. For despite what we have said about the more philosophic aspects of *Don Quixote,* it is in fact an extremely funny book. This brings us to another aspect of the Renaissance movement in Spain, as distinct from that in Italy or France, where serious

works generally were serious all the way. In Spain, humor was
blended with sadness—or even tragedy—not just for comic relief,
but as an integral part of the whole work. This is true in *Don
Quixote,* but in a unique way, since humor in this work grows
out of the pathos, and vice-versa. Note, for example, how fear
of the Don's anger makes Sancho's mirth even more irrepres-
sible, and how Don Quixote himself laughs through his own
melancholy. We can understand what Meredith meant when he
said that Cervantes' humor is "world-wide, with lights of tragedy
in the laughter . . . the richer laughter of heart and head in one."
Yet it is surprising that Cervantes himself denounced satire as
being "unworthy of a generous heart," since he himself had a
keen sense of satire. This denunciation on his part is explained
by his desire to harmonize the two elements of any one point of
view, and to counterbalance, say, realism and fantasy, or criticism and sympathy. His humor is never totally satirical, because
it is never totally cruel. Cervantes is not presenting Don Quixote
as an absurd object of mockery at the hands of the down-to-
earth Sancho. Cervantes, throughout the humorous dialogues
between the knight and his squire, is really indulging in a serious
internal dialogue between the two parts of his own nature. There
is even a duality of emotions in Don Quixote's death scene. For
in his very farewell to laughter and his expressed hope to see all
his friends soon in the next world, there is that unique mixture
of pathos and absurdity which makes our tears those of sorrow
and mirth at the same time. Cervantes achieves this by digging
into the very center of his characters. In all of us lie these twin
elements of joy and sorrow which are exposed in the creations
of Sancho and the Don. Cervantes penetrated deep enough in
Don Quixote, however, to show how the Don and Sancho in all
of us are not two clearly defined elements set against each other.
They are at once stable and flexible, volatile and stoical, tragic
and hilarious. The fact that Cervantes succeeded in unifying
them so brilliantly is ample testimony to his genius.

DETAILED SUMMARY OF *DON QUIXOTE*

PART ONE

CHAPTERS 1 - 4:   We are introduced to the main character of the book; a withdrawn, gaunt man, about fifty years old, who lives in a village in the province of La Mancha. He spends most of his time reading books on chivalry, to such an extent that he decides to become a knight-errant himself. Dressed in old, rusty armor—including a visor made of pasteboard—he mounts his old hack, whom he calls Rocinante, and sets out on his adventures, having given himself the title "Don Quixote." Before departing, he decides upon a farm girl who will be his lady, as in the romances. He gives her the title Dulcinea del Toboso. The first adventure on his expedition takes place at at inn, which he assumes to be a medieval fortress, where he meets two ladies of easy virtue. Imagining them to be ladies of the castle out for a stroll, he addresses them in the high-flown language of knight-errantry. He flies into a rage when they laugh at him, but the situation is saved by the innkeeper, who takes in Don Quixote. The Don feels sad at not having been officially knighted, and persuades the innkeeper to perform the ceremony. Just then, a carrier removes Don Quixote's armor from a trough —taken to be an altar—but is discovered by the knight-errant, who hits the thief over the head with his lance. The innkeeper, who does not want any more trouble, performs the ceremony of knighthood with the aid of one of the two ladies who, stifling her laughter, says the words: "God make your worship a fortunate knight and give you good luck in your battles." Properly knighted, Don Quixote proceeds on his way. His next decision is "to take into his service a neighbor of his, a poor laborer who had a large family, but was very suitable for the part of squire in chivalry." On his way home, however, he saves a young shepherd, Andrew (Andrés), from a beating by a farmer, then proceeds on his journey, leaving Andrew in the same predicament as before. He meets six merchants from Toledo, and, sensing an opportunity for a new adventure, demands that they swear his lady, Dulcinea del Toboso, to be

29

the most beautiful woman in the world. They demand evidence before they swear to this, whereupon Don Quixote flies into a rage and attacks them by way of defending the name of his good lady. They beat him up so badly that he cannot rise, which puzzles him, since he is a knight-errant. He decides that the disaster was the fault of his horse, Rocinante.

> **COMMENT:**   Cervantes wastes no time in setting the whole tone of the book by giving us a brief but complete portrait of Don Quixote, and by telling us enough about him to justify his later actions. Already anomalies in his behavior patterns manifest themselves. His conduct in leaving Andrew to the mercy of his assailant, after making a gesture of saving him, can be called into question. Yet his courage cannot be questioned, as shown in his single-handed attack on the six merchants. It is interesting to note how carefully Cervantes establishes the moral tone of the work. Don Quixote's mission has basically good motives, and we can immediately sense at least three views that might be taken of Cervantes' purpose in writing the work. The first is that, by making Don Quixote a thoroughly ludicrous figure, he is mocking the idealistic utopians who set out to right all the wrongs of the world. The second is that Cervantes is deploring the fact that a man with such a noble purpose is so rare that he does look absurd. The third is that he is obviously seeking some kind of value judgement on romantic chivalry and knight-errantry from within the historical context of his time. We notice, for example, how ridiculous his gallant gestures are toward Dulcinea, the lady of his choice, and toward the two women at the inn. Yet we cannot help observing that he is showing them a respect they probably never received from anyone else.

CHAPTERS 5 - 7:   Since Don Quixote is unable to stir, he decides to fall back on a device about which he had read in one of his favorite romances—that of singing a ballad under such circumstances. As he sings, a laborer from his village, Pedro Alonzo, comes to help him. The knight thinks Pedro is the Marquis of Mantua, a character in the romance from which the ballad was taken. Pedro tries to assure Don Quixote that he is his neighbor, and that the knight-errant is his friend, but is met with the answer, "I know who I am." Pedro is convinced that Don Quixote is crazy, and they return to their village, where there is an uproar because of Don Quixote's three day absence. His housekeeper tells the priest, Doctor Pero Perez, that all the books about knight-errants have turned the Don's brains, and that she has overheard Don Quixote talking to himself about becoming a knight. Don Quixote's niece then tells the barber, Master Nicholas, that she has seen her uncle finishing one of the books, then lashing out at the walls, after which he claimed that he had killed four giants. The niece then suggests that these books are dangerous, and should be burned as heretics, to which the priest agrees, adding that a public inquisition will be held the following day. Don Quixote is put to bed, where he tells them that his injuries are due to Rocinante's fall during a fight with "the most monstrous and audacious giants to be found anywhere on earth." Pedro then tells the priest about Don Quixote's ravings, which further prompts the churchman to take action. The following day, the priest and barber go through the knight's books, passing judgement on each one before either burning it, banishing it, or saving it. That night the housekeeper burns all the books that are left. The priest and the barber wall up the room in which the books had been kept and two days later the housekeeper tells Don Quixote that an enchanter removed them. The knight claims that he knows the enchanter, who bears the Don no personal malice, but merely wishes to prevent his performing further deeds of gallantry. The niece then suggests that Don Quixote should abandon his ideas of knight-errantry, and that he should stay in his village and lead a peaceful life. The knight starts to fly into a rage, so both the housekeeper and niece leave him alone. After fifteen days, during which time he insists to the priest and the barber that knight-errantry should be revived, he persuades Sancho Panza to become his squire, suggesting the possibility of the poor man's being one day governor of an island. Without bidding farewell to friends or family, they set out one night on their expedition, having raised a little money. Sancho reminds the knight about the island.

COMMENT: To begin with, the attitude of "normal" society is highlighted in this section by the attitude toward the knight shown by Pedro, the niece, the housekeeper, the barber and the priest. To them the knight is quite simply mad. Yet we must not forget that Don Quixote's attitude to them could well be identical. The conversation between the priest and the barber on the books and the consequent burning of the books by the housekeeper, apart from being hilariously funny, is an ironical comment by Cervantes on the Index of forbidden books and on the Inquisition. Note that the object of burning the books is to prevent other people from being affected by them, yet Cervantes is careful to point out that all these romances promulgate the virtues of life, such as honor, marital fidelity, and courageous action against the forces of evil.

It is clear too in this section that Don Quixote does not *think* he is a knight—he actually *is* one. Knight-errantry *is* the real world for him. Sancho Panza is introduced as a rather vaguely defined character, poor and "without much salt in his brain-pan." An immediate contrast is set up between him and Don Quixote, in that Sancho's motives in becoming the knight's squire are mercenary and based on worldly ambition, whereas the knight's reasons for setting forth are of a noble stamp, thoroughly idealistic and romantic in the tradition of medieval chivalric honor.

CHAPTERS 8 - 10:   Chapter eight begins with the famous incident of the windmills. Don Quixote and Sancho see thirty or forty windmills standing in a plain, and the knight immediately says they are giants whom he is going to attack. Sancho tries to dissuade him, but in vain. Don Quixote scorns Sancho's arguments, and urgees Rocinante forward at full gallop, issuing a war cry as he does so. Just then the wind turns the arm of the nearest windmill with such force that Don Quixote's lance is shattered, and the knight is toppled from his horse. He claims that his temporary setback was the work of the same enchanter who removed his room and books. They continue on their way, and Don Quixote starts teaching his squire, who has begun to gulp wine, some of the rules of knight-errantry. Under the influence of the wine, Sancho begins to see the adventures as pleasures, rather than work. After a night's sleep, they continue on their way. Don Quixote tells his squire to come to his rescue only if the rabble attack him, since there are certain social rules in knight-errantry that have to be obeyed. Then they encounter two Benedictine monks on horseback, accompanying a Basque lady in a coach, traveling to join her husband in Seville. The knight sees the monks as enchanters abducting a fair lady, and charges them in a spirit of gallantry, knocking one of the monks to the ground. Sancho proceeds to strip the monk of his clothing and tells the monks' two servants that the clothes are the spoils of battle. The servants beat Sancho, and the monks proceed on their way. Meanwhile Don Quixote is assuring the lady that he has saved her honor, but just then one of her Basque servants approaches the knight, who calls for his lady Dulcinea to save him. They again join battle, but Cervantes comments that he cannot tell the end of the story until he tells the reader about the original manuscript. Cervantes then disgresses by telling of how in Toledo he came across the original story of Don Quixote, which he says had been written by a certain Arabic historian called Cide Hamete Benengeli. The fight with the Basque ends in triumph for the Don, who agrees to spare his life at the lady's request only on condition that the servant go of his own accord to the lady Dulcinea, who will decide his fate. This section ends with a conversation between the knight and his squire in which Sancho reminds the Don of the island he had been promised. The squire suggests that no further punishment should be bestowed upon the Basque. Don Quixote agrees, congratulates the squire on his common sense, and ends by delivering a speech on his sense of utter dedication to knight-errantry.

COMMENT: The windmill incident is important as indicating through action the initial attitudes of the knight and Sancho Panza toward reality. The windmills *are* giants to Don Quixote, and they *are* quite obviously windmills to his squire. Cervantes could be telling us here that the "real" world rests in the eyes of the beholder. Shortly after this incident we have the first inkling of a breakdown in Sancho's role as the man of common sense, for under the influence of some wine he begins to see certain glamorous aspects to the world of chivalry. Sancho's apparently staunch position, therefore, is not impregnable. After the incident with the Basque, however, the servant-master relationship between Sancho and the Don is re-established even more pointedly by the squire's sycophantic attitude toward the knight. Sancho's dialogue shows common sense and a kind of earthy wisdom, coupled with a greed displayed by his constant reminding Don Quixote about the island he has been promised. Don Quixote, on the other hand, responds to Sancho's attitude—the squire continually refers to him as "your worship," for example—by adopting an air of pompous didacticism toward his servant. This section is worth studying for the relational aspects between the two main characters, and for the slight hints we are given that changes in their respective attitudes could conceivably take place.

CHAPTERS 11 - 14:   They reach some goatherd's huts, where they are greeted with hospitality, so they decide to spend the night. A brief conversation takes place between Don Quixote and Sancho, in which the knight condescendingly allows the squire to eat with him. Sancho momentarily objects to this "noblesse oblige" attitude, but Don Quixote forces him physically to set beside him, and, taking some acorns in his hand, proceeds to deliver a long harangue on the golden age of the past, of which the acorns remind him. A young muscian enters with his fiddle, and entertains the company with a charming Spanish ballad. Don Quixote wants to hear more, but Sancho objects because he is sleepy. Another boy enters and announces that a "famous shepherd-student," Chrysostom, died that morning, reputedly for the love of Marcela, the beautiful daughter of someone he calls "rich William." Chrysostom is awaiting burial, and the events leading up to his death are now recounted to us. Apparently Marcela had many suitors, but spurned them all and took to tending the flocks despite her wealth. The men of the village followed her—including Chrysostom, who is rich and handsome, and who writes poetry to her, some of which is quoted here. Chrysostom has now died of a broken heart, and Sancho and Don Quixote go to the funeral, and on the way the knight-errant delivers a lecture to the travelers on the inestimable virtues of knight-errantry. This harangue is delivered at the request of one of the travelers called Vivaldo, who, with the rest, has decided that Don Quixote is mad. The knight's speech on chivalry is historical in nature, dwelling on the heroic deeds of King Arthur, and of the other romantic heroes celebrated in literature. Vivaldo starts a debate with Don Quixote, arguing against knight-errantry on the grounds of its essential paganism, since these so-called heroes committed their lives to women, not to God. The knight contradicts this by saying that ladies certainly were invoked by these adventurers, but that they commended themselves first to God. The argument peters out after Vivaldo observes rather cynically that not all knights-errant were hopelessly enough in love to dedicate their lives to women, and that the process of shoving a lance through someone's body did not strike him as an action motivated by a love for God. The travelers reach the grave, where Vivaldo reads Chrysostom's last poem. Marcela appears and delivers a tedious dissertation on love and beauty. The section ends with the travelers inviting Don Quixote to go with them to Seville. He declines the invitation, saying that he has to clear the mountains of thieves and robbers.

COMMENT: The knight's attitude to Sancho during the meal, and Sancho's response, is an indication of the absurdity of the social dichotomy and human rapport between them. Don Quixote's "acorn speech" is undoubtedly Cervantes' way of ridiculing the overdone contemporary attitude of glorifying the past, an attitude prevalent among many humanists of the day. Note how the knight's inflatedly chivalric posture collapses temporarily when he wants to hear more music, which he has enjoyed thoroughly—as a human being, not as a knight-errant. The Chrysostom story shows the influence of the pastoral novel on Cervantes, and the knight's continual interruptions during the telling of the story is probably Cervantes' way of mocking the arrogant pedantry which was one of the more distasteful aspects of the Renaissance. The debate between Vivaldo and Don Quixote can be read almost as a dialogue Cervantes is having with himself on the religious and moral aspects of the chivalric tradition. There is a strong tone of parody in much of this section. The whole Chrysostom tale seems to be almost deliberately out of place here, which suggests an attitude of humorous criticism of the pastorals. The reading of Chrysostom's farewell poem is almost certainly a burlesque of the traditional funeral laments, while Marcela's defense of her actions, protestations of innocence, and harangue on love and beauty, contain all the elements of a melo-dramatic lampoon.

CHAPTERS 15 - 17: The knight and his squire enter the woods into which Marcela has disappeared. They cannot find her, and while they are having lunch Rocinante trots off to find some mares belonging to twenty carriers from Yanguas. The squire's nag is mauled by the mares and beaten by the Yanguesans, upon which Don Quixote and Sancho attack the carriers, who beat them mercilessly. The knight claims that this defeat was due to the fact that carriers are rabble, and takes the blame for having defied the laws of chivalry by demeaning himself. He orders Sancho to deal with rabble in the future, since a knight may join battle only with another knight. The squire now objects in earnest, saying that after the severe beatings he has received, he will never draw his sword again to defend any cause. Don Quixote comes away with another eloquent defense of knight-errantry saying that wounds are the honorable emblems of chivalry, They proceed on their way with the knight riding on Sancho's donkey, Dapple, Rocinante attached to its tail, the beaten squire leading the way. Two miles on they reach an inn, which the Don protests is a castle, of course, and there the knight is put to bed in a garret, where his wounds are tended by the hostess and her daughter. The garret is shared by Sancho, Don Quixote, and a carrier whom the maid of the inn has arranged to visit through the night. As she steals into the garret, however, Don Quixote, who has been dreaming of Dulcinea, imagines that the maid is his fair lady, seizing her and makes a gallant speech to her. The carrier, thinking himself deceived, pounces on the knight and beats him. The maid, in terror, leaps into bed with Sancho, who beats her. The innkeeper arrives, and a free-for-all ensues. An officer of the Holy Brotherhood is staying at the inn and, shocked by the proceedings, calls for the police. Things quiet down temporarily, and the Don tells his squire that the castle is enchanted, which is small consolation to the bruised Sancho. A policeman arrives, and the knight calls him a lout. The policeman hits Don Quixote with a lamp and leaves. Sancho wryly suggests that the policeman was undoubtedly a Moorish enchanter. At dawn, Sancho mixes a strange, liniment-like brew which the knight and he drink, both getting violently ill. Before they leave, the Don refuses to pay the innkeeper, claiming that the establishment was unworthy of a knight-errant He rides off, leaving Sancho to face the angry innkeeper, but just then some rogues seize the squire and toss him in a blanket. Don Quixote shouts insults at Sancho's tormentors and offers him some of his home-made liniment. The innkeeper keeps Sancho's saddle-bags as payment.

COMMENT: The hilariously bawdy scene in the inn is akin in spirit to something out of Fielding's *Tom Jones*. This section also shows a change in Sancho's attitude. His description of a knight-errant as one who ". . . is beaten up one day and made Emperor the next," for example, shows an increasing awareness of the harsh realities of the rough life he has chosen, while containing an indication of his own daydreams of power and glory. The blanket-tossing scene is an important commentary on the characteristics of the Don and Sancho individually, and an indication of a breakdown in their relationship. When the knight realizes, for example, that "it was *only* his squire shouting," he does not come to his aid, displaying his speciously chivalric reason for covering up his fear. Note that the Don is really courageous when he is genuinely a medieval knight-errant; when he slips momentarily into his contemporary real-life role, he displays normal fears. This temporary change of role is indicated also by the fact that "had it not been for his rage, he would certainly have burst out laughing." Sancho, too, is not unnaturally disgruntled by his treatment by the rogues and his abandonment by Don Quixote. There is a mingled tone of despair, sarcasm, Chaplinesque resignation, and almost cynical self-mockery in his cry to Don Quixote: "Has your worship forgotten, by any chance, that I am not a knight?"

CHAPTERS 18 - 21: Sancho, thoroughly disgusted and disillusioned with this life of knight-errantry, makes up to Don

Quixote; He tells Don Quixote this in no mean terms, but the
knight insists that his squire has much to learn about the honor
of winning chivalric battles, to which Sancho agrees—because
they haven't won a battle yet. As they continue the debate, two
clouds of dust appear in the distance, which Don Quixote interprets immediately as being made by two oncoming armies,
They are, in fact, two flocks of sheep. The knight's description
of the golden armor, the shields, emblems, and squadrons of
many nations is quite superb, and the reader senses the mounting excitement as they lie in wait upon a hillock to join battle.
Sancho then tentatively suggests that there may be some delusion involved, but the knight attributes the squire's scepticism
to fear, insisting that Sancho listen for the neighing of horses,
the blaring of trumpets, and the beating of drums. Just as the
squire insists that all he hears is the bleating of sheep, Don Quixote spurs his nag, tilts his lance, and charges. Altogether he kills
seven sheep, and the shepherds retaliate by pelting him with
stones, removing some of his teeth. The knight drinks some of
the liniment and vomits over Sancho, who vomits over the Don
in return. Sancho now complains about having been tossed in
the blanket and having lost his saddle-bags, but Don Quixote
comforts him by assuring him of God's mercy. Sancho in turn
is solicitous over his master's loss of teeth and the pair continue
on their journey with good relations restored. They come across
mourners carrying a bier on which is a corpse, assumed by
Don Quixote to be that of a knight. Seeking revenge on behalf
of the unknown knight, he charges the mourners, breaking the
leg of one churchman. It is at this point Sancho describes Don
Quixote as the Knight of the Sad Countenance. They find their
way to a meadow, where they hear clanking noises, which the
knight wants to investigate. Sancho prevents this by hobbling
Rocinante. Sancho tells the Don a senseless story about the
exploits of an unattractive shepherd and shepherdess which the
knight impatiently interrupts. It is discovered that the clanking
noises come from six fulling-hammers which make regular
pounding and clanking sounds. Sancho starts to make fun of
the Don, who hits the squire twice with the lance in anger, and
lectures him on the danger of familiarity. They continue on
their way and meet a barber in the rain with a brass basin
covering his head, which the knight takes to be Mambrino's
golden helmet. At the end of this section, Sancho shows some

solid wisdom in advising Don Quixote to employ his talents in some worthwhile cause.

COMMENT: This section starts with Sancho's first open rebellion against the way of life into which Don Quixote has led him. Yet notice how the squire is immediately wooed into the knight's world by the sheep incident, showing how Sancho can slip as easily into the world of romantic chivalry as Don Quixote. The marvelous description of Crusade-like heraldry and pomp in this passage shows how steeped Cervantes was in a romantic literature, and the description has an exciting appeal about it that suggests that the author himself had a nostalgic affection for the world of chivalry, The humane, compassionate side of Don Quixote's character is also brought out in these chapters. When Sancho complains about the way he has been treated, there is a tenderness in the knight's response which is genuine and humane. The knight is also sincerely apologetic and contrite for his maltreatment of the churchman, and the religious flavor of his sorrow has often been pointed out as Cervantes' own personal statement of his belief, Sancho's pseudo-pastoral tale is an almost overdone parody on this art form. There is a very interesting change here in both the knight and his squire. Don Quixote actually recognizes the hammers as being hammers, and assumes an almost Sancho-like attitude to this fact. Sancho, on the other hand, assumes an air of almost romantic wisdom in his advice to the knight. Here we have the first traces of the role-switching process.

CHAPTERS 22 - 26: Don Quixote and Sancho meet a chaingang being taken off to the galleys. The knight questions them on the reasons for their punishment, and after listening to their tales of woe, some of which are rather spicy, he decides that they should be freed. He attacks a guard, and when the convicts free themselves, the knight orders them to report to his lady, Dulcinea. A spokesman for the group, Gines, refuses to do this, giving very sensible reasons for his refusal, whereupon the knight becomes furious, attacks them, and is stoned. Don Quixote and Sancho now go to a wooded, mountainous area called the Sierra Morena, where the escaped convict, Gines, steals Sancho's donkey. They then find a leather bag containing finery, money and writings. The knight reads a love poem and a letter from the bag, but they give no clue as to the identity of the owner. They see a figure leaping around in the distance, and set out to find him. En route, they meet a goatherd who tells them the story of a young man who had appeared some time ago looking for a remote place in which he could dwell, apparently as some kind of penance. At one time this young man had attacked a goatherd, in a fit of madness. Sancho and the Don find the young man, whose name is Cardenio, and who is the figure they had seen prancing around earlier. He is called the Ragged Knight of the Sorry Countenance by the Don. Cardenio tells his story. He came from a rich family, and had loved a beautiful girl called Lucinda, also wealthy. On the day Cardenio's father was to have asked Lucinda's father for a wedding, however, an Andalusian grandee had requested that Cardenio be the companion to his son, Don Ferdinand. Don Ferdinand loves Dorothea, a rich peasant girl, and arranges a ruse whereby he can leave his father to see the girl. The ruse works, but after Don Ferdinand promises to marry Dorothea, he satisfies his physical passion and leaves her. The story continues with Don Ferdinand's falling in love with Lucinda, and Cardenio's jealousy, but at this point in the story Cardenio goes into a kind of fit, attacks Don Quixote, and disappears. The knight and the squire start out to find him, but Sancho again says he wants to quit this life and go home. This is really an excuse to start a long dialogue with the knight, who had chided Sancho earlier for talking too much. After much conversation and musing on his role as a knight-errant, Don Quixote decides to lead a life of hardship as a hermit for awhile, and sends Sancho to Dulcinea with a message of assurance of the knight's enduring, courtly love for her, Sancho reaches the inn where they had stayed earlier, and meets the priest and barber from the village. They decide to rescue Don Quixote from his hermit's life and devise a plot whereby the priest will become a damsel-errant and the barber will be her squire.

COMMENT: There are obviously autobiographical aspects to Cervantes' introduction of the galley slaves. In the original Spanish, there are many puns in their stories, but these cannot be captured in translation. Don Quixote shows a genuine sense of humanity in helping them to become free, and one cannot help feeling a sense of injustice in his being stoned, despite his bizarre conduct, Cervantes is making a severe comment here on the vicious judiciary system of 16th-Century Spain. There is some bad organization in Cervantes' plot in this section. At one point, the escaped convict steals Sancho's donkey, and a page or so later the squire is getting off it, and a little later the donkey disappears, with no explanation. Cardenio's story in this part is an excellent example of a good chivalric tale taken from folk-lore and fitted smoothly into the main story. It is continued further on, however, and is at times overdone and out of place. There is an interesting comment by Don Quixote on his own mental state when Sancho threatens Dulcinea with physical violence if she does not express her love for the knight: " . . . As far as I can see, you are no saner than I am." Sancho's conduct when confronted by the priest and the barber can be interpreted either as a face-saving pose or as an attitude prompted by his dream of the island. The latter interpretation is probably true. The "damsel-errant" device is a hilarious burlesque of the whole chivalric concept.

CHAPTERS 27 - 31: The priest and the barber proceed to execute their plan by borrowing clothes from the landlady and dressing up. As they set out, led by Sancho, the priest has scruples about a churchman's being dressed as a damsel, so they decide to switch roles. As they approach Don Quixote's hermitage, the priest and barber decide to persuade the knight to become an Emporer, which would be more advantageous to him than becoming an Archbishop. Just then they hear a beautiful song being sung by someone who turns out to be Cardenio. The young hermit finishes telling his story to the priest and the barber. Apparently, despite his jealousy, he had decided to ask for Lucinda's hand, but did not want to offend his own father. Don Ferdinand had offered to help, sent Cardenio away, and then had asked for Lucinda's hand in marriage for himself from her parents, who agreed, since he was such a good prospect. Cardenio had spoken to Lucinda before the wedding, and she had told him she was obliged to go through with it.

Cardenio had watched the wedding ceremony from a hiding place. After saying "yes," Lucinda had fainted, a letter had been found on her, and Cardenio had run off half mad. After he finishes his story, they find a shepherd "boy" sitting by a stream. This turns out to be Dorothea, the girl in Cardenio's story whom Don Ferdinand had promised to marry and then deserted. Dorothea, who does not know Cardenio, tells her side of the story. After Don Ferdinand's desertion, Dorothea, having learned that he had married Lucinda, ran away from home to confront him with his conscience. Apparently the letter Cardenio had seen being taken from Lucinda said that Lucinda was already married to Cardenio, making marriage to Don Ferdinand impossible. Don Ferdinand had tried to kill Lucinda, and Dorothea had now taken to the woods on hearing that her father was under the impression that she had eloped with one of his servants. She says that Lucinda had entered a nunnery. After this, Sancho finds Don Quixote half dead with hunger, but refusing to return to Dulcinea until he has proven himself worthy of her. Dorothea volunteers to play the role of damsel-errant to get the knight to go home. She succeeds in bluffing the knight, and they get under way. Much dialogue takes place, during which the priest tells of having been robbed by galley slaves, and curses their liberator, who unknown to him, was Don Quixote. The knight trounces Sancho, who has suggested that Dorothea is more lovely than Dulcinea. Sancho sees his donkey being ridden by the galley slave, Gines, shouts, and retrieves it. Sancho again annoys Don Quixote by describing Dulcinea as she really is. Andrew, the boy Don Quixote had saved and deserted, appears on the scene and begs the knight not to help him ever again.

COMMENT: Cervantes is poking fun at the ecclesiastical structure here by having a priest try to get Don Quixote away from his hermit's life in case he becomes an Archbishop. Sancho's worldly ambitions are added to the satire when he says: ". . . So far as bestowing favors on their squires went, Emperors could do more than Archbishops-errant," Cardenio's resumption of his tale seems redundant at this point, and this part of the story is in any case over-romanticized. Dorothea's part of the story is as beautiful and poignant as the first portion of Cardenio's. Cervantes is obviously inconsistent in his handling of this convention. It is interesting to note the priest's inhumane attitude to the man who liberated the galley-slaves and thus ". . . rebelled against his King and natural lord, for he acted against his legal authority." Cervantes is here upholding one of his own religious positions, namely, that the Christian's moral obligation to the welfare of his unjustly treated fellows takes precedence over legal authority *if* that authority contravenes the ethical code to which the Christian is bound in the name of God. The conversation between Cardenio and the priest is important in two respects. First, Cervantes is virtually saying that he himself will be considered a genius if he can successfully portray the bizarre character of Don Quixote. Secondly, the priest's comments on the anomalous nature of the knight's rational and irrational behavior are at the core of any discussion of the character of Don Quixote.

CHAPTERS 32 - 35: The party eventually returns to the same inn which has appeared in previous sections. A great deal of talk takes place, including details of how to get Don Quixote back home. While the knight is asleep, the conversation gets around to books on chivalry, which the innkeeper says he enjoys. A debate follows, in which the priest selects two of the innkeeper's books for potential burning. Although Sancho takes no part in the debate, he is a fascinated bystander. One of the tales under discussion is called *The Tale of Foolish Curiosity,* and a large part of this section is taken up with the priest's telling the story. The tale is centered around two friends, Anselmo and Lothario. Anselmo marries a girl called Camilla and asks Lothario to woo her in order to test her loyalty. Lothario is unwilling to do this, but sees a great deal of her on Anselmo's insistence, the result being that he falls in love with her. One night Lothario sees the lover of Camilla's maid leave the house, and thinks that Camilla is being unfaithful to him. Madly jealous, he tells Anselmo that Camilla is about to be unfaithful, and they arrange that Anselmo will listen in hiding when Lothario and Camilla next meet. He repents of having told Anselmo, and confesses to Camilla what he has done. They play a trick on Anselmo by assuming the roles of ardent wooer and virtuous, faithful wife, with Anselmo listening. The husband is fooled, and Lothario resumes his love affair with Camilla. At this point, the priest's reading of the story is interrupted by Sancho, who rushes in to tell them that Don Quixote is having a battle. The knight is indeed having a battle —in his sleep—and is slashing the inn's wineskins, believing that he has met a giant, and that the wine is blood. There is a general commotion, but eventually the knight and his squire are quieted down, and the priest resumes telling the story. One night Anselmo hears noises coming from the maid's room (her name is Leonela) and finds her lover leaping from the window. The maid pleads with him not to discharge her, promising him that she will tell him wondrous things. Anselmo tells Camilla about the incident, and Camilla, knowing that her affair with Lothario is going to be exposed, runs off with her lover. Anselmo goes to hear the maid's story, but she too runs off, leaving him wifeless, friendless, and servantless, all because of his own suspicion and curiosity. He dies of a broken heart in a friend's house. Lothario is killed in battle and Camilla enters a nunnery. When the priest has finished telling the story, he complains about the incredibility of a husband being as stupid as Anselmo was.

COMMENT: The debate on the book seems to be another self-dialogue by Cervantes, and it is interesting to note Dorothea's comment on the innkeeper's attitude to romances: "Our host is not far short of being a second Don Quixote." The tale recited by the priest is a good example of the romances so popular in Cervantes' day. Sancho's character is worth examining in this section. While listening to the debate on the books, he is momentarily disillusioned about the value of knight-errantry. Yet he still harbors hope that the world of fantasy can lead to the reality of worldly power. Notice how the audience, entranced by *The Tale of Foolish Curiosity,* is interrupted by Sancho's tale of the Don's fight with the giants. The listeners themselves are immediately translated into the knight's unreal world of real fantasy. At this point, the reader is made aware that Sancho is in a state of transition between his down-to-earth sense of reality, and the world of knight-errantry. When he tells the guests, for example, that he must find the giant's head, we believe

he has totally entered Don Quixote's world. Yet there is
the possibility that he is adopting a tongue-in-cheek attitude to the whole business both to save face and to sus-
tain the possibility of earning an island, The priest's
comments at the conclusion of the story could well be
Cervantes' own comment on the official ecclesiastical attitude to morality in literature. The priest's attitude is that
such conduct is credible between lover and mistress, but
preposterous between husband and wife.

CHAPTERS 36 - 41:   At this point in the story, four horsemen and a lady arrive at the inn. The horsemen have lances,
shields, and black masks, and the woman is dressed in white,
with her face covered. Dorothea veils her face and Cardenio
hides in Don Quixote's room. The lady in the group appears
very sad. It turns out that the lady is Cardenio's Lucinda and
one- of the horsemen is Dorothea's Don Ferdinand. After a
prolonged discussion and a great deal of weeping and wailing,
the couples are reconciled and everyone is delighted—except
Sancho, who has been under the impression that Dorothea was
a real princess. The squire wakes up the Don and tells him that
the fantasy is over, that the giant was a wineskin, the blood
was wine, and the princess is in fact an ordinary woman called
Dorothea. Don Quixote wishes to see these transformations for
himself, but after talking to Dorothea, who informs him that
things *are* as they were, the knight berates Sancho for lying to
him. The next character to appear in the book is a gentleman
who has apparently been living with the Moors. His lady, a
beautiful Moor who desires to be a Christian, is with him.
During dinner, Don Quixote discourses at great length on the
differences between the man of letters and the man of war,
ending with a bitter attack on the gross banalities of the contemporary age. The gentleman, Ruiz Perez de Viedma, is then
asked to tell his story, which is known as *The Captive's Tale*.
Viedma was one of three sons whose father bade them enter
three professions: war, the world of business, and scholarship.
Viedma chose war, and tells a rather tedious story about battles
with the Moors, and so on. He and some others are captured.
A wealthy, beautiful Moorish girl who once had a Christian
maid and now wishes to be baptized herself promises to rescue
them. A long, elaborate plan is drawn up, and she gives them

money to ransom themselves and buy a ship. They do this and take her with them, intending to return to Spain. En route they are pirated, however, and lose nearly all of their money. The girl's name is Zoraida; she wishes to be called Maria. Viedma is now in very bad straits, and is looking for his father or brothers. It turns out that the judge who shortly arrives at the inn is Viedma's youngest brother, the one who chose learning, and the story ends with a moving reconciliation between the two. It is interesting to note that in the middle of the tale, Cervantes himself is mentioned as being one of the captives: "... a Spanish soldier, called something de Saavedra." Cervantes makes highly laudatory comments about his own courage in captivity.

COMMENT: In view of the question of Sancho's attitude raised in the previous section, it is interesting to observe his conduct with Don Quixote here. With the others, he plays the role of medieval squire; now, however, he is the down-to-earth peasant, again temporarily disillusioned. Note Don Quixote's boundless enthusiasm, however, and how it woos the reader—as well as Sancho —back into the world of his illusions. We sense too that Cervantes is really speaking through the mouth of Don Quixote when the knight deplores having to live in "such a detestable age as we now live in." For, as we have discussed, Cervantes was acutely aware of the vices as well as the virtues of his age. Even here, however, the knight-errant shows inestimable optimism in stating, "If I achieve my purpose, I shall be the more highly esteemed for having faced greater dangers than did the knights-errant of past ages." As a side comment, it should be noted that this statement is a rebuttal to Turgenev's contention that Don Quixote is not egotistical. *The Captive's Tale* is interesting from several points of view. Despite its tendency toward tedium, it gives a good idea of the hardships of the prisoners' lives. Furthermore, it shows the influence of the Moorish novel on Cervantes, as well as giving us some interesting autobiographical details. The theme of conversion from Islam to Christianity is a commentary on one of the religious aspects of 16th-Century Spanish life.

CHAPTERS 42 - 46: The judge mentioned in the previous section arrives at the inn, and after the priest tells him some of Viedman's story, recognition and reconciliation take place. The judge's daughter, Clara, accompanies him, and there is a mule-lad, who is really a gentleman, who follows the judge's train through love for her. The innkeeper's daughter and her maid play a trick on Don Quixote by tying his hand to the bolt of the hayloft door. At dawn, four travelers come to feed their horses. The noise wakes everyone up, Rocinante, on whom the Don was mounted, moves away from the door, and Don Quixote is left dangling until the maid unties him. Don Quixote explains it all by saying he is enchanted again. The four travelers have come to take the mule-lad back to his father, and an argument ensues. The innkeeper's wife asks Don Quixote to help make two guests pay their board, but the knight says he must ask Dorothea before he undertakes any more noble deeds. He receives permission, but refuses to fight the men when he discovers they are not knights. Meanwhile the judge is talking to the mule-lad, Don Luis, and has found out about his love for Clara. He says he will try to arrange something, Now the barber arrives who had worn the basin Don Quixote took to be a helmet. He demands his basin, and Don Quixote is outraged, protesting that it is not a basin, but a helmet. A free-for-all takes place, with everyone joining in, but the knight succeeds in stopping it. An official now presents a warant for the knight's arrest for having freed the galley slaves. Another fight takes place, settled this time by the priest and the barber. All the love issues in the story are now settled amicably. Don Luis will accompany the judge and his daughter, Clara, and Dorothea and Don Ferdinand are determined to get Don Quixote back to his village by continuing the ruse that was being used before. Sancho again expresses the opinion that Dorothea is not a real princess, for she is always kissing Don Ferdinand. Don Quixote flies into a rage at Sancho, but Dorothea quiets him by saying that it must be the enchantment at work again. Now the priest, the barber, and other members of the party devise a way of getting the knight home without any further help from Dorothea and Don Ferdinand. The men put on disguises, truss up Don Quixote and put him onto a wagon inside a cage. By way of consolation, the barber delivers a lofty, rhetorical, and allegorical speech about the matrimonial union of a lion and a dove. This indeed soothes the knight, who interprets the speech as meaning that he will be married to his lady Dulcinea. Don Quixote ends this section by praising Sancho for his loyalty and by reminding him of the gift—an island—which will be the squire's reward. The knight is carried off by the "enchanters."

COMMENT: This section is spoiled by involved plot complications, contrived identity disclosures, and unnatural reconciliations. There is little cohesion here, and the digressions become tedious at times. Nevertheless, this section does shed some interesting light on the Don and Sancho. The knight's specious arguments against fighting the two guests remind us of the incident with the Yanguesans. Yet he cannot be accused of being completely cowardly, since he has shown physical courage on other occasions. His relations with Sancho are worthy of some study. The knight shows admiration for the squire when he tackles the barber, even saying that Sancho is worthy of receiving the order of chivalry. On the other hand, Sancho's attitude to Dorothea sends Don Quixote, the *knight,* into a rage; Don Quixote, the *person,* however, shows a tenderness toward Sancho when he says of him: "For I know the poor man's goodness and innocence too well to believe that he would make false accusations against anyone." It is almost as if, at this point, Sancho's relationship with the knight is real only in the world of the Don's fantasy, and Don Quixote's attitude to his squire is human only on the level of Sancho's reality. Although Cervantes says of Sancho that "he was not far from sharing his master's disease," Sancho is at this point deliberately opting for the Don's world because of the ever-present dream of his island. Yet when he enters that world, we have the definite impression that he is as comfortable there as in his own.

CHAPTERS 47 - 51: Don Quixote is carried off in the cage, and Sancho is unsure of what position to take in the affair until a Canon joins them and questions the whole issue. The knight protests that he is under a spell, and the priest—in disguise— backs up the Don's argument by assuring the Canon that this man is in fact the enchanted Knight of the Sad Countenance.

At this point Sancho objects, saying that the realities of life have to be faced, and pleads with the disguised priest to abandon this world of illusion. At lunch, Sancho tries to dispel the Don's illusions about being enchanted, but in vain. The knight is adamant in maintaining that he has been caged by enemies of knight-errantry. There then follows an interesting debate between the priest and the Canon on the question of the absurd contents of fiction and drama. An amusing scene follows between Sancho and the Don, in which the squire tries to bring the knight back to reality by suggesting that after such a long confinement, Don Quixote might possibly want to relieve himself by performing certain bodily functions to which petty mortals are prone. The knight does so, but insists still that he is enchanted, The Canon then suggests to Don Quixote that his madness is probably due to his having read so many romances, to which the knight gives a very clever and pointed retort. Sancho pleads with Don Quixote to try to escape from the cage, and the knight agrees. Shortly after this, the squire defends his ability to govern the island he hopes to earn for his chivalric endeavors. A goatherd runs up chasing a she-goat, and during a brief discourse with the priest, the goatherd asserts that peasants learn their philosophy through exeperience. He then tells his story, which is known as *The Goatherd's Tale*. Leandra, the most beautiful girl in a local village, is wooed by all the local boys. Neither she nor her father can decide whom to choose. The two main suitors are Eugenio—the goatherd telling the tale —and his rival, Anselmo. While the father is trying to make up his mind, an egotistical, pompous adventurer arrives in the village full of exaggerated stories of his warlike exploits. His name is Vicente de la Roca, and he is in fact poverty-stricken, but so charming that Leandra runs off with him, taking her father's jewels. Vicente then steals her money and finery and deserts her in a cave, leaving, however, her honor intact. Her father banishes her to a nunnery until the scandal dies down, and the suitors all resume their daily tasks in the fields tending the goats, and so on. Anselmo weeps over Leandra's absence, while Eugenio despises her and curses women for their fickleness.

COMMENT: Sancho once more lapses into disillusion about his earthly ambitions and is disgusted at having to return home a failure. Note how the priest's conversation

with the Canon suggests that the priest himself has been
temporarily drawn into the world of romance, and is
enjoying it. This factor has already been seen in the innkeeper's attitude to chivalric literature, in Dorothea's role,
and, of course, in Sancho. Don Quixote's return is quite
symbolic, for here we have the world of romance caged
and dragged into the mundane world. The priest plays
Devil's Advocate in his debate with the Canon when he
accuses religious literature and drama of transporting
audiences into a dream world. Note also the insight and
brilliance of Don Quixote's response to the Canon's arguments, which shows that within the realm of fantasy the
knight is sane, rational, and logical. The knight's argument that the Canon himself could be accused of leading
an enchanted life, and that ecclesiastical authority has no
right to challenge the deep-rooted heritage of chivalry,
seems to be coming from Cervantes himself. Sancho's
claim that he is perfectly capable of ruling an island is
interesting. Cervantes is here challenging the feudal conception that only those born of noble stock are capable
of assuming a role of leadership, The reader's appetite is
whetted here, and we wonder how Sancho would in fact
fare, were his dream to come true.

CHAPTER 52 AND VALEDICTORY: At the end of the goatherd's tale, Don Quixote announces that he, in the true tradition
of knight-errantly, would have righted all the wrongs that took
place in the story. The goatherd makes a comment about Don
Quixote's foolishness, whereupon the knight hits him in the
face with a loaf of bread. A fight breaks out, which stops when
a trumpet is heard; the sound comes from a group of penitents
bearing an image of the Virgin Mary. Don Quixote immediately
sees an opportunity for a new adventure and, mounting Rocinante and bearing his shield, he calls out that in the chivalric
tradition he is going to rescue the good lady who is obviously
being abducted by rogues. As he charges them, Sancho tries to
dissuade him from such an irreligious act. Sancho pleads in vain,
however, and the knight orders the penitents to release the
beautiful lady, who, he says, is being taken off against her will,
since there is a look of sorrow on her face and there are tears
in her eyes. The penitents take him to be a madman and burst

out laughing, which sends Don Quixote into a rage. He draws his sword, attacks them, but is knocked to the ground. Everyone, including Sancho, thinks the knight is dead, and the squire delivers a tearful eulogy over the prostrate figure. Sancho's mournful words arouse Don Quixote, who begs to be placed on the cart. Sancho agrees immediately, and suggests that they return to the village, where they will be able to plan new adventures. As they arrive at the village, Sancho's wife, Juana, runs up to meet them, asking her husband if she may see all the finery which he has brought home for her from his adventures. Sancho dismisses her pleas almost with contempt, assuring her that on earning his island, she will enjoy the inestimable honor of being called "Your Ladyship." This happens to be a perfectly delightful conversation. Don Quixote's niece and housekeeper weep and wail over the catastrophes that have befallen him, and the priest instructs the niece to ensure that the knight will not escape again. This sends the women into torrents of vitriolic abuse against the authors of all the books which caused his madness. Cervantes concludes Part I by saying that he has been unable to find out anything more about the knight, but that he found some Valedictory Poems, which he gives us. They consist of three epitaphs on Don Quixote, and three sonnets on Dulcinea, Rocinante, and Sancho Panza. He ends by promising more of the knight's adventures once they have been unearthed by scholars.

COMMENT: Critics have come away with several interpretations of Don Quixote's attack on the penitents. Some say that Cervantes is here pouring open scorn on the adulation accorded the Virgin Mary by the Roman Catholic Church. Others claim that, as a loyal Catholic, he is defending what the Virgin Mary represents against abuse by the superstitious and the ignorant. What cannot be disputed is the absolute honesty of Don Quixote's motives, particularly when he sees the tears in the Virgin's eyes. Sancho's eulogy is worth studying. To begin with, he is obviously grief-stricken at the thought of his master's apparent death, and, absurd as it sounds, there is a certain poignancy in his addressing the "dead" knight as a "flower of chivalry" and "glory of your race." Then, with quite sudden brilliance, Cervantes brings everything into perspec-

tive by having Sancho exclaim, "O liberal beyond all Alex-
anders, since for only eight months' service you have given
me the best isle surrounded and encircled by the sea." So
by now Sancho has indeed accepted his role in the dream
world of knight-errantry, but with his own private dream
forever before his eyes. He has also assumed much of Don
Quixote's resilience and powers of recovery, for note how
rapidly he accepts the fact of the knight's being alive, and
how bouyantly he anticipates a new set of adventures.

PART TWO

GENERAL COMMENTS: It was Cervantes' original plan to
expand the 1605 version of Don Quixote into four separate
parts. This was never executed, however, and the whole work
consists of two sections. Part II was published in 1615 and,
of course, the time lapse had certain marked effects on this
portion of the work. Cervantes himself had obviously mellowed,
a change shown in such aspects of the second part as the
increased air of majesty about Don Quixote and the sagacity
of Sancho Panzo as governor of the Isle of Barataria. Yet
while there is a more philosophic tone to Part II, and while
Cervantes shows a surer and more deft touch in his treatment
of much of it, there is somehow a lack of the sparkle and
sponteneity which continually appears in Part I. There is also
a change in the relationship between the knight and the squire.
The tone of this change is set by the scene in chapter ten in
which Sancho arranges for the Don to meet Dulcinea. Don
Quixote on this occasion sees Dulcinea and the other farm girls
for what they really are, while Sancho insists that this means
the Don is enchanted, since the girls are princesses. The knight
finally succumbs to his squire's argument. There is an apparent
switch of roles here, with the Don as the man of reality and
Sancho as the man of fantasy. This reversal is not completely
authentic, however, since Sancho still has his eye on the governorship of his island, and is not above a practical joke.

Another example of the differences between the two parts is
the horseplay in Part II—particularly in the scenes with the
Duke and Duchess—which seems much more heavy-handed
and less genuinely hilarious than before. As far as construction

goes, the second part is extremely confused and ill-planned, with many digressions, disjointed incidents, and long digressions, in which it is often impossible to find one clearly outlined theme. There are nevertheless many aspects to Part II which are worthy of close study, and many passages of brilliant writing. We shall now examine these aspects separately in the light of what we already know of Don Quixote and Sancho Panza, their characters and motivation, and Cervantes' purpose in writing the novel. First, however, a general outline of the plot will give the student an idea of the framework in which Cervantes dealt with his themes and treated his subject matter.

CHAPTERS 1 - 10: After Don Quixote reveals his desire to go on his adventures again, the barber tells him a story with a moral attached to it which is directed at keeping Don Quixote home. Sancho then goes into the details of what the villagers think of the knight, pointing out to Don Quixote the varying opinions which the inhabitants have of him. Sancho also gives the knight the rather surprising bit of information that a history of their adventures has been put out about them by a Moor and a sage. One of the villagers, the Bachelor Sampson Carrasco, corroborates the fact that their story has been published. Sancho, Don Quixote, and Sampson discuss the history, the possibility of their going on further adventures, and other topics. In the fifth chapter, Sancho's wife is told that he is going off on his travels again. There is an argument, of course, followed by tears, but Sancho leaves nevertheless. In the following chapter, Don Quixote informs his niece and his housekeeper that he is about to proceed on new adventures, and this news is also followed by an argument. Then Sancho arrives to help plan their expedition. In chapter seven, Sancho and Don Quixote make detailed arrangements for their proposed adventures. Don Quixote's housekeeper tells Sampson that the Don is leaving and pleads for his assistance in restraining him and Sancho. Sampson offers his helmet to the knight, and is roundly cursed by the housekeeper for this.

The knight and his squire set out to see Dulcinea, and have a conversation on the way. This is a short dialogue on the respective virtues of the religious and the chivalric life. They then have an argument over Dulcinea, in the course of which Sancho admits that he never did go to see her. Chapter Ten opens up the new phase in the relationship between the knight and the squire already referred to in our introductory comments. Note the subtlety and cunning of Sancho's argument here. One would imagine that he would be taken off guard by the Don's sense of reality, but he uses this as proof that the knight really *is* under a spell, just as the Don has used the appearance of reality against him in Part I. It is interesting also to see how Sancho plays on the fact that the Don is missing a great deal of beauty by seeing Dulcinea and the two girls as they really are, and not as princesses.

CHAPTERS 11 - 20:   On the way, the pair come across an acting company. The actor playing the "Devil" scares Rocinante and Dapple, for which prank Sancho wants to wreak vengeance on the company. Don Quixote forbids him to do so, which is another indication of the apparent switch in their roles. This is a particularly interesting scene, since the actors do represent a kind of artistic fantasy world to which one would imagine Don Quixote would respond. In Chapter Twelve, this apparent reversal of roles is actually brought to light in a short conversation between the knight and the squire:

> "Every day, Sancho," said Don Quixote, "you grow less simple and wiser."

> "Yes," replied Sancho, "for some of your worship's wisdom must stick to me."

Shortly after this, they meet the Knight of the Wood, who is grieving over a lost love. There then follows a conversation between Sancho and the Knight of the Wood's squire, in the course of which Sancho says of his master: "I mean there's nothing of the rogue in him. His soul is as clean as a pitcher. He can do no harm to anyone, only good to everybody. There's no malice in him. A child might make him believe it's night at noonday. And for that simplicity I love him as dearly as my heart-strings, and can't take to the idea of leaving him for all his wild tricks." Of all the commentaries one could make on the deepening relationship between Sancho and Don Quixote in Part II, and on the sincere love which the squire develops for his master, none could match this one in its eloquence and simplicity. In Chapter Fourteen, the Knight of the Woods claims that he has previously conquered one Don Quixote, apparently not knowing whom he has just challenged. The Don expresses doubts about such a fight, and they decide to settle the matter by having a duel. While the Knight of the Wood is getting horsed, Don Quixote attacks him and knocks him to the ground. It turns out to be Sampson Carrasco, who also goes under the name of Knight of the Mirrors because of his shining armor. Apparently the Bachelor, together with another villager called Thomas Cecial, who acts as his squire, has set out in the guise of a knight to get Don Quixote to return home. After this incident, Sampson and Thomas have a discussion in which the latter makes the following interesting observation: "Don Quixote's mad, and we're sane. Yet he gets off sound and smiling, while your worship comes out bruised and sorrowful. So let's consider now which is the madder, the man who's mad because he can't help it, or the man who's mad by choice?" It is interesting to note how synthetic Sampson and his squire appear—despite the apparent sanity of their mission—compared with Don Quixote and Sancho, who have an apparently insane mission but who yet come through as authentic.

Don Quixote now encounters someone called Don Diego with whom he discusses such topics as knight-errantry, the education of children, and poetry. Next follows one of the most hilarious episodes in the whole book—the encounter with the lions. To prove his bravery, the knight urges a lion-keeper to allow the lions out so that he may fight them. The keeper, protesting, opens one cage, but the lion yawns, looks out of the cage, ignores the knight, then turns around and lies down out of sheer boredom. To Don Quixote this constitutes a great triumph. Yet for all the absurdity of the scene, it should be noted that the knight stood his ground, and was indeed prepared to encounter the lion. This is another example of his complete absence of fear when *totally* in the role of knight-errant. Don Quixote and his squire now arrive at the home of Don Diego, where they meet his wife, Doña Christina and his son, Don Lorenzo. Don Lorenzo and the knight have a long conversation about poetry. In Chapter Nineteen a student starts telling the true story of two men, Basilio and Comacho, both of whom love a girl call Quiteria. Comacho wins her and Don Quixote and Sancho are present at the wedding festivities.

CHAPTERS 21 - 30: The same story is continued. As the vows are being exchanged, Basilio thrusts a dagger into himself, demanding as his death wish that Quiteria give him her promise to be his wife. She does so out of pity, thinking he will die anyway. It turns out that Basilio has tricked the company, however, and a fight ensues which Don Quixote stops. He earns the esteem of everyone present, particularly for the words of sage advice which he delivers. It is interesting that this is the kind of romantic tale which would have been *related* in Part I, whereas in Part II it is actually acted out. As a historical note, it should be mentioned that there had been objections to the plethora of romantic stories superimposed upon the narrative of Part I. Cervantes therefore decided to reduce these in Part II, and where he did introduce them, to interweave them more into the fabric of his tale. Note too than Don Quixote now has an opportunity to actually play a real-life part in a romantic scene, and he plays his part nobly. From Chapter Twenty-two to Twenty-four we have the famous Montesinos' Cave, which we will summarize in detail later. Don Quixote wishes to see the cave, and Sancho lowers him down into it. After a time, the squire becomes anxious and hauls his master out. Don Quixote meanwhile has had a vision, and in one of our essays later we will discuss Cervantes' use of this device. In Chapter Twenty-four there is an apologia for the Montesinos' Cave incident.

We are next told the story of a man who lost his donkey, and of how he and a friend went out braying to lure it home. They found it dead, and other people made their lives miserable by imitating their braying, We now have the incident of the Prophetic Ape, who assures Don Quixote that the vision in Montesino's Cave was half true and half false. The pair attend a puppet show depicting scenes "from French chronicles and Spanish ballads." They see a tableau re-enacting the routing of the Moors, and Don Quixote gets caught up by the story, destroys the puppets, and has to pay for them. It turns out that Peter, the puppetmaster, is in fact Gines, the leader of the galley slaves in Part I. Don Quixote and Sancho then come across two villagers fighting over the braying incident cited above. Don Quixote gives them a lessen in theology; Sancho brays for the fun of it and gets knocked out. Sancho now takes Don Quixote to task for deserting him after being knocked out by the villagers, but the knight smooths things over in the same way as he did on several occasions in Part I.

Don Quixote now finds a boat; Sancho and he climb in and it takes them to a mill, which the knight presumes is a castle. The millers pull both of them out, knowing that the mill would grind them up, as in fact it does the boat, for the loss of which Don Quixote pays sixty *reals*. He still demands that the prisoners of the castle be set loose. The knight and the squire now meet the Duke and the Duchess, who have heard of the adventurers through the previously published history.

CHAPTERS 31 - 41: We are taken to the Duke's estate, where Sancho tells a rather malicious story about who sits at the head of the table. A quarrel breaks out between Don Quixote and a priest, who has chastised the knight for having left his estate. In Chapter Thirty-two, during a discussion on Sancho's potential merit as a governor, Don Quixote says of his squire: " . . . I would not exchange him for any other squire, even if I were to receive a city to boot; and therefore I am in doubt whether it would be right to send him to that governorship with which your Higness has favored him. . . ."

At this point the Duke and Duchess begin to play tricks on Don Quixote for their own amusement. During one conversation, Sancho tells the Duchess of their adventures, after which she and the Duke go to a great deal of trouble to get people to play the different characters who had taken part in these adventures. It is all of the cheap practical-joke caliber, and Cervantes seems to be using a reverse picaresque technique in order to ridicule the asinine behavior of which the upper class of his day was capable. Sancho is finally granted his governorship by the Duke and Duchess.

CHAPTERS 42 - 51: Sancho talks a great deal about his island, saying such things as: "Ever since my journey through the sky, when from its lofty height I gazed on the earth and saw it so small, my very great desire to be a governor has partly cooled. For what greatness is there in governing on a mustard seed?" At another point he says, "Let them dress me as they will . . . for whatever way I go dressed I shall be Sancho Panza." Don Quixote then gives Sancho some lengthy advice, ending with the words: ". . . I consider you worthy to be governor of a thousand isles. You have a good instinct, without which all knowledge is of no avail." Sancho then leaves to be governor of his "isle," and Don Quixote broods after his departure.

We now have the portrait of Sancho as governor, displaying the wisdom of Solomon in matters of dispute. At this point the Duke and Duchess play another one of their pranks on Don Quixote, which leaves him prostrate for five days. Meanwhile Sancho is doing a superb job as governor, settling arguments, making good laws, and generally giving an impression of innate powers of wise leadership. Sancho receives a letter from Don Quixote commending him on his good job, and Sancho replies.

CHAPTERS 52 - 61:   Sancho's wife writes to both Sancho and the Duchess, and Sancho leaves his job as governor. The practical jokes which have been commissioned by the Duke are more than he could take. After one last practical joke has been played on him, the knight leaves the castle for good. Don Quixote and Sancho Panza resume their relationship, and have a long conversation about this. Then the knight, seated upon his nag, waits on a road for an adventure to come along. Most opportunities simply pass him by, but eventually he is successfully trampled upon in the traditional way. The knight and his squire now come across an inn, which Don Quixote actually calls an inn, not a castle.

In Chapter Fifty-nine Cervantes makes a very pointed reference to the false Part II which we have already discussed. En route to Barcelona, they are both robbed, and there is a temporary breakdown in the relationship between the two, in the course of which Don Quixote threatens to whip Sancho. The amount of the adventures with the robber is particularly long and tedious. They eventually enter Barcelona, where they immediately get into a brawl with the natives.

CHAPTERS 62 - 74:   They stay with Don Antonio, who

plays tricks on them, though less malicious ones than those perpetrated by the Duke and Duchess. Two nobles have rigged up a bronze bust which apparently can speak. It does, and says, as did the Ape, that the Cave vision was half false and half true. There now appears a character called the Knight of the White Moon, who jousts with Don Quixote on conditions that if the Don loses, he will be punished by having to spend a year at home. Don Quixote loses, and Don Quixote has to spend six days in bed. The Knight of the White Moon turns out to be Sampson Carrasco again, and Don Antonio's comment to the villager concerning Don Quixote's return home is particularly interesting: "May God pardon you the injury you have done the world in your attempt to restore the most amusing of all madmen to his senses. Don't you see, sir, that no benefit to be derived from Don Quixote's recovery could outweigh the pleasure afforded by his extravagances?" Sampson then goes home.

After Don Quixote's recuperation, he and his squire set out for home, during which we have more examples of Sancho's increasing wisdom. Don Quixote is desperately trying to make Sancho flog himself in order that Dulcinea may be disenchanted. In Chapter Seventy an interesting commentary is made by Cervantes on the Duke and Duchess, when he says that they were "within a hair's breath of appearing fools themselves for taking such pains to play tricks on a pair of fools." Don Quixote, in desperation, promises Sancho that he will add a hundred *reals* to his wages if he will flòg himself in order that Dulcinea may become disenchanted. Sancho reluctantly agrees, and whips himself. Yet another reference to the bogus Part II is made in Chapter Seventy-two. As the pair approach home, Sancho sees his wife. Shortly after arriving, Don Quixote takes to his bed, where he reaches sanity again. He makes his will, part of which states that his niece will lose her inheritance if she marries a man who reads books of chivalry. He then dies.

SOME ASPECTS OF PART TWO OF *DON QUIXOTE*

1. PUBLIC OPINION AND PART II: The first part of *Don Quixote* was so popular that the public made several demands on Cervantes, demands which he virtually had to obey to survive as a writer. Much the same thing happened to Shakespeare, who re-introduced Falstaff into *The Merry Wives of Windsor* because of the public outcry at the character's reported death in *Henry V*. In Cervantes' case, the public wanted more funny actions on the part of Don Quixote and more ludicrous sayings from Sancho Panzo. Yet the reader finds that he has grown tremendously fond of these two characters from having met them in Part I, and somewhat resents the maltreatment and indignities to which they are subjected in Part II. Their conversation and general discourse is, of course, as delightful as ever. Yet we get the impression at times that Cervantes suddenly remembered his obligation to his reading public, and forces some dire catastrophe to happen to his two characters. The second part almost has the effect of a melodramatic and disastrous crescendo, for everything seems to happen to the knight and his squire. They are pinched, beaten, ducked in water, trampled by bulls, and generally mauled unmercifully. There are two ways of looking at this, of course. Left to his own devices, Cervantes might well have avoided much of this and stuck to the same vein he employed in the first part. On the other hand, it could be that he thought some kind of retribution should be meted out to his characters for their outrageous presumption.

2. DEFENSE OF PART II: In our introduction to Part II, we outlined some criticisms of this section on the grounds that it does not have much of the sparkle, freshness or ingenuity of Part I. Yet some critics say that the second part is superior to Part I. They say, for example, that some of the funniest incidents in the whole book are centered on Sancho's governorship of Barataria, or on incidents like that of Countess Mafalda in the Duke's castle. These champions of Part II, claim, for example, that although some of the practical jokes played by the Duke and Duchess may be on the extravagant side, at least they are ingenious. But the main virtue of Part II, according to these critics, is the fact that its essential literary value does not depend on exterior action, but on inner motivation. It is, in other words, more profound and philosophical. Since Cervantes identifies himself—and undoubtedly mankind—with both Sancho and the Don, he has drawn them closer together. This is shown, for example, in the deeper nature of their discourse, by their growing dependence on each other, and by the interchange of attitudes toward reality and fantasy which they manifest in their conversations and behavior.

3. REALITY AND UNREALITY: We first see Sancho as a blunt, plain, down-to-earth character who bases his life on what is normally called hard reality. He has an intelligence born of experience, and his experience exists in believing only what he sees. He is certain that he can rely on his good common sense to offset the fantastic whims and delusions which beset his master. He is sceptical about everything which does not satisfy his immediate sense of reason. There is no place in his philosophy for the occult, the fantastic, or the theoretical. We feel, however, that Sancho is probably willing to accept the fact that there *are* indeed things that cannot be known. When he moves into the Don's world, he knows what he is about, namely that by playing the game, he will gain worldly power. For awhile, all the arguments which Don Quixote brings to bear upon him have apparently little or no effect. Every time an enchantment is thrown in his face, he recalls the beatings he has received, or the humiliation of the blanket-tossing incident.

What happens in Part II, however, is that almost unwittingly Sancho himself becomes a kind of bewitcher. He pretends to have visited Dulcinea at Toboso, for example, and thereby draws Don Quixote into the world of fantasy for a change. It is clear that the squire loves his master for his child-like simplicity and naivete, and he openly states that a child could convince the knight-errant that noon is night. But as soon as Sancho begins to use this knowledge, he gradually slips into the world of fantasy himself, as is shown in the scene when he insists that the three farm girls are in fact princesses riding on palfreys. He has become Don Quixote. And when Don Quixote says, "They are donkeys," he has become Sancho Panza. Irrespective of his motive—the island—he is now using the world of fantasy to try to combat Don Quixote, to outwit him at his own fantastic game. But his very refusal to go all the way with this fantasy means that when he pits his sense of enchantment against the knight's, Don Quixote wins because of the totality of his belief. Note, for example, how he begins to doubt whether the Knight of the Shining Mirror's squire *is* his neighbor Cecial, once Don Quixote starts persuading him that he is seeing visions.

One of the most interesting confrontations in the whole book is that between Don Quixote and Sancho Panza over the knight's vision in the cave of Monesinos. At first glance, this is the old Sancho of Part I, the down-to-earth peasant, pouring scorn on the world of fantasy. And again, Don Quixote's position seems to be that of the crazy man living in a world of illusion. But if we examine this scene more closely, we see that their positions have in fact been reversed. For the knight is believing the evidence of his senses, and Sancho is contradicting him by saying that it was all the work of enchanters. What actually happened was that Don Quixote's imagination took reality into a new dimension—but it remained reality. This is the sense in which the Ape's verdict that the vision was false *and* true, was accurate.

4. THE CAVE OF MONTESINOS: SUMMARY: Don Quixote has heard a great deal about the cave of Montesinos, which is in the province of La Mancha, The cave is reputed to contain many marvels, and the knight-errant expresses a strong desire to see it. A well-known local scholar is assigned to guide the knight and the squire, and after saddling the horses the party sets out. They lodge that night in a village six miles from the cave, and buy 150 feet of rope, since Don Quixote insisted on seeing the bottom, even if it reached hell. The following day they reached the mouth of the cave, where the scholar and Sancho tie the rope around the knight. Before entering, he prays to God for guidance and begs Dulcinea for protection. As he hacks his way through the undergrowth leading to the cave, a great number of crows and jackdaws bowl him over. Don Quixote is a good Catholic, however, and not superstitious, otherwise he might take this as a bad omen. As he is lowered into the cave, Sancho shouts a blessing and crosses himself many times. Don Quixote shouts back that he wants more rope, After half an hour, the scholar and Sancho pull up the rope, and know that the knight is now at the bottom, But suddenly, with about thirty feet of rope still to go, they feel a weight at the end and gradually make out Don Quixote. He is unconscious when they get

him to the surface, but they shake him so heartily that eventually he wakes up, looking around him as if in alarm. The knight chides them for having robbed him of the sweetest vision that any human being has ever beheld, and proceeds to recount to them what happened.

About twenty feet down there was a concave, which he entered to rest for awhile. Gathering the rope into a coil, he sat down and wondered how he could reach the bottom without any support. He then fell asleep and found himself in a beautiful meadow when he woke up. Suddenly he saw a crystal castle out of which came an old man wearing a purple cloak, and carrying a rosary. He embraced the knight, introduced himself as Montesinos, and said that the inhabitants of that enchanted place had been waiting for many centuries for Don Quixote's arrival. The knight was to see the marvels contained in the castle, and was to tell the world about them. Don Quixote asked Montesinos if the story was true that Montesinos had cut out the heart of his friend Durandarte and presented it to the lady Belerma. Montesinos said that the story was perfectly true. The Don was then led into a low, cool hall in the castle, where he saw a sepulchre on which a knight was lying with his right hand resting beside his heart. Montesinos tells Don Quixote that this was Durandarte, who had been enchanted, together with Montesinos himself and many more knights and ladies, by the French wizard, Merlin. No one knows why they were enchanted or why Durandarte, having been killed by Montesinos, occasionally complained and sighed as if he were alive.

Just then, Durandarte cried out in anguish, reminding Montesinos that it was he, Durandarte, who had requested that his heart be cut out and taken to Belerma. On hearing this, Montesinos fell to his knees and admitted it, adding that Belerma was also in the cave, enchanted by Merlin. He told how not one of the enchanted had ever died, although some had been transformed into lagoons. Durandarte's squire, Guadiana, had been changed into a river, which still ran with sorrow at his master's death. Montesinos ended his speech to Durandarte by telling him how the renowned knight-errant Don Quixote had arrived, and that through him they might all become disenchanted. Just then the Don heard loud screams and, turning his head, saw a procession of lovely maidens filing past in mourning. Behind them walked a lady dressed in black, beetle-browed and shrivelled, bearing a cloth which contained a heart. Montesinos told Don Quixote that the ladies were servants of Durandarte and that the lady was Belerma. Don Quixote ends this part of his story by saying that Montesinos had compared Belerma's former beauty of that of Dulcinea. He now proceeds with the second section of his tale.

Don Quixote then saw three peasant girls frisking in the beautiful meadows. He recognized one of them as being Dulcinea and the other two as her friends. Montesinos said he did not know them, but was certain that they were ladies of quality who had been enchanted recently by Merlin. The Don spoke to Dulcinea, but she paid no heed to him and ran away. Montesinos then told the knight that it was pointless chasing her, that it was time he returned to earth, and that he would be informed later as to the method of disenchanting them all. At that point, however, one of Dulcinea's friends had approached Don Quixote with a request for money on Dulcinea's behalf. The knight expressed surprise to Montesinos that the enchanted could possibly need money, to which Montesinos replied that this was a universal problem. Don Quixote had only four *reals,* which he gave to the girl with instructions for Dulcinea that he craved her company and would devote his life to releasing her from her enchantment. The girl took the money, but instead of thanking him, said that the Don owed more to Dulcinea, and instead of making a curtsey, she pranced and leapt in the air.

CHARACTER ANALYSES

DON QUIXOTE: Many varied interpretations have been given of the character who, having steeped himself in mediaeval romances, dressed himself in rusty armor and cardboard helmet, and set out on his nag, Rocinante, in the role of knight-errant. On one simple, straightforward level, of course, he can be viewed at best as a simple-minded buffoon, or at worst as a completely raving lunatic. In fact, the only adventures he meets with are a few ludicrous mishaps, and on this same level he is just an old fool who permits himself to be the dupe of practical jokes. But is he merely the hero of some burlesque, the cruel object of our scornful laughter? It is probably true to say, as has been suggested, that Cervantes put a tremendous amount of his own self into his creation, and that there are in Don Quixote symbolic and allegorical profundities of characterization which perhaps were not intended, but which are there nonetheless. This makes him one of the most puzzling and fascinating creatures in literary history, and the only certain judgment that can be made on his character is the fact than we cannot be definitely certain of all its implications.

The knight is indeed an absurd figure. But in any appraisal of his character, we must examine him in the light of what is meant by absurdity. Albert Camus, in his *Myth of Sisyphus,* saw the legendary Sisyphus as being in an absurd predicament, which the French intellectual related to man and his dilemma. And in some ways there is a certain similarity in the ludicrous situation of both Sisyphus and Don Quixote. The one rolled a stone up and down a hill eternally, and the other charged windmills. But both did so in divine terms, one as punishment by the gods and the other as a one-man messianic stand against the great forces of evil that beset the world. Don Quixote can well be depicted as a Christian hero, setting forth to right the wrongs of the world by his own bizarre methods. Seen in this light, he is an absurdly noble figure, a triumphant failure in a deeply religious sense. The forces of evil at which he tilts his lance are too huge, too gross, and too static for him to conquer. In this way he represents the Christian existential humanist, the celebration of man who sets himself up as a force greater than those forces around him. Don Quixote has carved out a unique space for himself in the universe of his own creation and fantasy, and his mission is the divine one of salvaging the world from banality and torpidity. He fails, of course, in the most pathetic ways possible. There are two ways of looking at this failure. He could represent Cervantes' way of lauding the humanist hero despite his failure. The great impersonal forces which Don Quixote attacks are in many ways impregnable, but at least the knight at no time loses hope or personal dignity. He is, in fact, the only truly noble character in the whole book, despite his absurdity. Seen in this way, his failure is really a victory, since he leaves the signature of his personality behind him wherever he goes, whereas the duchesses and innkeepers of his world seem paltry in comparison. Cervantes may, therefore, be telling us that we must not stifle the Don Quixote in us, that we must set forth to seek the answer to the unknowable and venture into the world of the mysterious. Otherwise we shall lose our sense of divine purpose completely and eke out our lives in banality.

The other way of looking at Don Quixote's failure is to see it as Cervantes' statement of the utter, ludicrous hopelessness of such divine ventures. Why? Because the very word "divine" is a concept which is totally meaningless when we attempt to translate it into terms of reality. The religious hero, the saint, the mystic, the utopian, are all living in a dream-world of absurd fantasy which is totally devoid of meaning or purpose in the mundane realities of daily existence. Such altruistic people have noble qualities, to be sure, just as Don Quixote has; they are courageous, virtuous, and generous-minded, just as the knight is. But what does their attitude bring them in the end, when they face up to the realities of existence? It brings them what it brings Don Quixote when he emerges from his fantastic world into the world of truth—namely, death. The knight is safe so long as he remains in his dream world, but when he wakes up, he has quite literally nothing to live for. There was an almost mystical joy in his role as knight-errant, just as Camus recognized a strange, almost indiscernible joy in Sisyphus.

In this way, Don Quixote, as an existentialist figure, does in fact inhabit the real world. His world of fantasy is fantastic only because shopkeepers and innkeepers see it that way, but we must remember that the knight's world is as real to him as the wine cellar is to the innkeeper. Seen in these terms, Don Quixote in fact poses the eternal philosophical question of the nature of truth and untruth, reality and fantasy. It is important to note in this respect the fact that he has deliberately *chosen* to inhabit the world which we would normally call "insane." But in so doing, he is merely moving into what could well be another dimension of reality, one which is beyond the ken of "sane" minds. Mention should be made here of Turgenev's essay on Don Quixote and Hamlet, since the Russian, by making this comparison of the two men, opened up new possibilities of our attitude to Cervantes' creation. Turgenev claims that both figures represent two diametrically opposed human positions, but mellows this interpretation by allowing that they are never in fact attained, but that they are positions toward which human nature veers. It is true that the two characters are opposite in that Don Quixote has a set, determined purpose and Hamlet vacillates. Yet they are extremely similar inasmuch as they are absolutely isolated figures, although set in entirely different social contexts and human predicaments. Yet Don Quixote is a Hamlet-like figure in many respects, inflated to preposterous dimensions. Although he obeys all the rules of chivalric ethics in his attitudes, he is the supreme egotist of literature. His dreams and fantasies are absurd parodies of Hamlet's introspective soliloquies, and his purpose is the noble one of destroying evil, the monstrous Claudius of his imagination. His wanderings, driftings and petered-out attempts to come to grips with his great impersonal enemy are much more closely allied to Hamlet's vacillations than Turgenev suggests. And when he dies, he leaves behind Sancho as a kind of bizarre Fortinbras, prosperous and triumphant in a pathetic kind of way. Even the death of Hamlet and Don Quixote can be seen in a similar light, contrary to Turgenev's thesis. For in becoming "sane" at the end, Don Quixote has merely returned to the insanity of the world he left, and it virtually kills him. Could not the same be said of Hamlet? In any case, viewed in its widest philosophical and metaphysical dimensions, the character of the knight of the "Doleful Countenance" poses at least as many puzzling problems as that of the "melancholy Dane."

On a more historical level of perception, the knight can be seen as either the symbol of all that was righteous in the chivalric ethic, or all that was deplorable in it. Perhaps Cervantes is using Don Quixote here to laud the virtues of a tradition that had in fact died out, and to point out that all the glories which that tradition embraced have no place in the banalities of contemporary values. There is also the possibility that the knight is a caricature, not only of the Erasmism of the Renaissance, but of the Sir Galahad of Medievalism. For Don Quixote is bookish and he is romantic. But we must again repeat the undeniable fact that he is absurd, and what Cervantes meant by this absurdity is an almost insoluble problem. One possible compromising solution is that Don Quixote, by his fantastic attempts to live the role of knight-errant, is in fact smiling the Middle Ages away, as Lord Byron said. But as he does so, there is an undeniable air of sadness and nostalgia in his comic gesture of farewell. The knight's brief moment of self-generated glory could be at once the twilight of Medievalism, the noon of the Renaissance, and the morning of modern times. It is not absolutely essential to imagine that Cervantes was passing any definitive judgement on the times by drawing the character of Don Quixote, or taking a positive stance either way. In many respects, Don Quixote the character stands pretty much for what *Don Quixote* the work does. They both represent a blending of the fantastic and the simple; a mixture of past dreams and present realities; a huge, funny, and sad testimony to the end of an era.

This last analogy can be carried even further. For in many ways, both the character and the novel can be viewed as symbols of human, literary, and historical optimism. They are both larger than life, and both are drawn on a gigantic scale. In no way must Don Quixote be regarded as some kind of medieval Walter Mitty, although both are brilliantly depicted literary types. While Walter Mitty is every man, Don Quixote is Everyman. We leave James Thurber's character with the feeling that while his delusions are of a grand nature, Walter Mitty isn't, quite simply because he isn't meant to be. Moreover, Walter Mitty's deeds take place entirely in his mind. We leave Cervantes' knight, however with the feeling that not only are Don Quixote's fantasies huge, but also that he himself is a huge personality. The great difference is, of course, that Don Quixote translates his dreams into action; not only that, but he also *becomes* a knight-errant. Therein lies his magnificence and his pathos. The optimism of both the novel and the character is a factor often omitted in analyses of both, but it is a feature worth considering. For by weaving the rich tapestry of the Middle Ages into the fabric of the Renaissance, and by pouring the picaresque into the mold of medieval romance, Cervantes set the tone for a new era of literary history. And Don Quixote's life and death should not be viewed as a failure. In many ways the world failed Don Quixote. His expeditions into the past failed, but they succeeded in pointing to the future. In Hegelian terms, his quixotic thesis clashed with the antithesis of a cruelly realistic present. But from this emerged a synthesis on which future hope can rest. It was in this state that he died. Unlike Falstaff, however, Don Quixote did not babble of green fields as death approached. He had already seen his green fields, and had charged over them with the determined gleam of medieval glory in his eyes. And when those eyes closed, they closed on a world that was gone, but in so doing they open our eyes to a world that lies ahead.

SANCHO PANZA: It is almost impossible to give any critical analysis of the "long-legged" rustic's character without placing him in continual juxtaposition to Don Quixote. The traits of his character, his attitudes to life, and the changes which take place in his personality all evolve from his continual conversations with the knight and his reactions to Don Quixote's activities. In one respect, he is a clear-cut character set in opposition to his master in certain ways. Contrary to Don Quixote, he is greedy, selfish, sane, and has a kind of native intelligence. Yet in some ways the differences are on a surface level, for the characters interact with each other and act on each other in such a way that almost a switch of positions takes place. Sancho too has an aim and an ideal at which he is aiming. His ambition is on a much more mundane level than the knight's, however, being centered on worldly power and wealth. Immediately we are again faced with the problem of the nature of reality and unreality, common sense and fantasy. It is easy to hold up Sancho as an example of the man who faces up to the realities of life. But is he to be admired outright for this, if the realities he seeks are no more noble than the acquisition of material goods and power? Furthermore, Sancho is as much an idealist as Don Quixote, and this is made particularly evident when he begins to feel the surge of chivalric glory which has gradually been transferred to him by his master. Sancho does not remain a static figure in any way; he changes, and as he changes he grows in stature. He starts off by being a stage stooge for the squire, but as the repartee of the drama proceeds, the stooge attains a certain wisdom somewhat more dignified than the earthy type of knowledge he brings to the scene.

It must be made clear that objective judgement should not be passed on the respective merits of either position. The critic who starts talking in terms of the "rightness" or "wrongness" of Sancho's attitudes is on dangerous grounds. For in many ways Sancho is just as universal a figure as Don Quixote, representing the failings, loyalties, selfishness and hopes of humanity. In modern psychiatric terms, Sancho can even be depicted in the relationship as one part of a split personality, the part which faces up to life as it really is. It is interesting to note, however, how he gradually works his way into being the Don's equal, and even ends up by being his superior in a ludicrous kind of way. One must never forget, too, the comedy of *Don Quixote,* and for the most part it is Sancho who provides the humorous touches. There is also a consistent quality in his character despite his hesitations, scepticism, and vacillations. The difference between him and Don Quixote in this respect, however, is that we always seem to know how the knight will act, but we are never quite sure about Sancho. Yet when the squire does act, we have the feeling that he really could not have acted otherwise. Another thing to remember is that Sancho's humor comes from within him, as Cervantes depicted him; in other words, we do not laugh at him through his wife's eyes or through his master's, but rather through the eyes of his creator. We know, for example, that Sancho will strike some ludicrously funny postures when he takes charge of Barataria. Yet toward the end of the book, despite some of the hilarious scenes, the reader gets the impression of an increasing seriousness in Sancho's attitude, illustrated by a growing closeness to Don Quixote which contains some moving elements.

In general terms, then, it can be said that Sancho is intended at first to symbolize the common man who sees things as they really are, unromanticized and unglamorized. Cervantes probably started off by intending to make Sancho nothing but a humorous scoundrel, and he is indeed a flimsy figure when we first encounter him. His wisdom, expressed usually in proverbs, increases as the book progresses. The final portrait in purely human terms is that of a peasant, ambitious in a material way, deceptive yet naive, untutored yet intelligent. The reader almost gets the impression that Cervantes grew to love his creation, as seen in his increasing dignity and sagacity in Part II. There is also the feeling at the end of the book that Cervantes meant Sancho's prosperity to be something thoroughly deserved.

THE MINOR CHARACTERS: Don Quixote and Sancho Panza tower above the rest of the 667 characters in this novel. In the true tradition of the picaresque novel, they are of infinite variety, and give a superb cross-section of 16th-Century Spanish society, from innkeepers, priests, students, and shepherds to the Knight of the Green Overcoat. On a more aristocratically romantic note there are characters like Camila, Dorothea, Fernando, Anselmo and Lotario. And of course there is Dulcinea del Toboso, elected by Don Quixote as his Queen of Love and Beauty.

One remarkable feature about the novel is that it does not have a heroine, for Dulcinea remains a somewhat vague, shadowy figure, placed there to serve a minor function. There are many women in *Don Quixote,* but none of them plays any real major role. Don Antonio's wife, for example, is called discreet, lovely, and gay, but Cervantes leaves us with that description and nothing more. We are told that Camila is the summation of virtue and beauty, but she never comes to life. Dorothea could have been a delightfully drawn character in a lower social context, but becomes trite and positively wearisome in the position she holds. Cervantes seems much more at home with characters of peasant stock; and the old gypsy woman, Don Quixote's housekeeper, and Sancho's wife, Teresa, for example, are drawn with swift, bold, and often humorous strokes. Again, the duke and duchess, despite their social stature, are dwarfed in characterization by the knight and his squire. One might object to the accusation that Cervantes was not too happy in his portrayal of upper-class types by pointing to the Ingenious Knight and the Gentleman in the Green Cloak as being well drawn characters. It should be pointed out, however, that these two characters are of humble birth. In short, Cervantes does a good job of drawing peasant characters, but becomes stilted and conventional when dealing with more aristocratic characters.

One possible reason for this is the fact that Cervantes was used to living in a lower-class environment, and was therefore more at home with the types associated with it. A more valid explanation, however, is that Cervantes found the aristocratic way of life too stilted and confining in reality to be able to do much with it in fiction. Furthermore, we must not forget that women in 16th-Century Spain lived an extremely cloistered existence, and even a man of perception did not have much scope to probe the feminine personality. Spanish writers of the day, therefore, depicted stock types of female characters, often not in a very flattering way. They were usually depicted as proud, fickle, jealous, garrulous and foolish. It is not really surprising, then, that Cervantes does not bring much life to his female characters, especially as they rise in the social scale, when they become more and more shadowy and insipid. Although the duchess talks more than Teresa, Sancho's wife is much more alive to us as a person, for example. Don Quixote's housekeeper has much more credibility in her portrayal than does Don Quixote's niece. For in the women of the peasant class, Cervantes found more depth and individuality formed by their deep-rooted, earthy sense of heritage.

BRIEF SUMMARY OF THE MOST IMPORTANT MINOR CHARACTERS

GINES DE PASAMONTE is one of the chain-gang convicts condemned to the galleys. Although rescued by Don Quixote, he and his fellow criminals stone the knight. His character is important for highlighting the pathetic absurdity of the knight in performing a deed of chivalric honor.

ANTONIA QUIXANA, Don Quixote's niece, is a very flimsily drawn character. Probably her most important function in the novel is that of being the recipient of unique instructions in the knight's will, whereby she must not marry a man who reads chivalric romances.

ROQUE GUINART is a character introduced by Cervantes to provide an ironic side comment on knight-errantry. An ill-fated character, he has become a bandit and captures the Don and Sancho. They attempt to turn him into a knight-errant, but he scorns their offer by turning them over to another bandit as amusement value.

DOROTHEA is a rather melancholy, erratic figure who poses as the traditional type of damsel in distress in order to try to persuade Don Quixote to return home.

DULCINEA DEL TOBOSO is the earthy type of peasant girl whom Don Quixote adulates in the traditional courtly way by making her the regal personification of love and beauty. He even bestows that title upon her, her real name being Aldonza Lorenzo.

MASTER NICHOLAS is the barber of the village. In an attempt to persuade the knight to go away from the Sierra Morena, he dresses up in woman's clothes and pretends to be Dulcinea. He also helps in the burning of the books.

THE INNKEEPER runs the roadside tavern which Don Quixote takes to be a fortress. He is a rather boldly drawn, credible character who serves a useful function in exposing Don Quixote's ludicrous posture. It is he who gives the Don the title of "knight."

ANDREW, although a very minor figure, is worth remembering the person whom Don Quixote temporarily rescued from receiving a beating. This is important since it was the knight's first wholehearted trial at performing a righteous deed in the name of chivalry.

THE FRIARS, who are introduced as escorts for the aristocratic lady, beat up Sancho Panza after Don Quixote, believing them to be abductors, storms the squire and his entourage.

THE CARTER is important as being in some way involved in the only really successful venture which Don Quixote has in the book. He is delivering caged lions to the king from the Governor of Oran, and the knight manages to outface one of them.

SAMPSON CARRASCO is a well-drawn character who, in the disguise of Knight of the White Moon and the Mirrors, finally overwhelms Don Quixote and orders him to give up his role as knight-errant, and to return home. He is quite an important figure symbolically, for after Don Quixote's rejection of knight errantry and death, we realize how flimsy Carrasco's pose as a knight has been compared to the Don's magnificent, though absurd, rôle.

THE DUKE AND DUCHESS are very vapid characters who play practical jokes on Don Quixote and Sancho Panza after inviting them to their home. It is they who create Sancho governor of the "island." It is interesting to note that these two noble characters come through as being devoid of personality, when compared to the knight and his squire.

ROCINANTE AND DAPPLE are the nag and the donkey who carry Don Quixote and Sancho Panza, respectively, through their outlandish adventures.

QUESTIONS AND ANSWERS

GENERAL COMMENTS: Cervantes' novel, *Don Quixote,* has over the centuries been the subject of much debate and controversy. It can be viewed, criticized and analyzed from so many different angles that no definite statement can be made which completely satisfies the demands of literary criticisms. Some critics have approached the work as a defense of time-honored institutions against the attacks of unrealistic reformers. Others see it as a monument to man's individual efforts to overcome the stagnating forces of history. It has been praised by medievalists as a permanent tribute to the noble attitudes and dignified postures which the Middle Ages sponsored. Another school of medievalists has attacked it as the work which mocked these attitudes and postures, causing the collapse of a rich and fertile tradition. Some people scorn the universal symbolic approach, claiming that it is to be read purely in a contemporary context, as Cervantes' ironical commentary on the passing social, political and ecclesiastical scene. It has been severely criticized for its disorganized, rambling construction, and lauded for the intricate complexities of plot, characterization, and theme. However one looks at it, *Don Quixote* still stands as one of the world's greatest masterpieces. We shall now give the student some ideas on which to base his future study of the work. Some of the viewpoints expressed here are deliberately contradictory, in order to expose the student to some example of the complex variety of opinions which Cervantes' work has evoked.

1. Discuss briefly the extent to which Cervantes' ideas were typical of contemporary Spanish thinking.

ANSWER: There are two clearly defined attitudes which can be adopted toward this question.

The first is that it was quite plainly *not* intended in any way to be satirically critical of any revered aspect of traditional Spanish institutions, such as the monarchy as embodied in Philip II, the Church, or contemporary politics. There is no esoteric or symbolic meaning behind the work, and it is to be regarded merely as a rollicking, hilarious tale of human failings, containing none of the sadness seen in it by such critics as Sainte-Beuve. It is a story written by someone who has gathered a great store of wisdom and experience, and who invokes the reader to distrust the imagination, to accept life as it is, and to take men for what they are worth. There is no need to penetrate the surface of Don Quixote's character to relish it. In this respect, and in others, it should be regarded as very Spanish. It incorporates two main characteristics of the Spanish temperament and mentality: on the one hand, an adventuresome spirit tainted with egotism and a kind of mystic idealism; and on the other hand, a spirit of practical positivism coupled with a romantic fatalism. The work is also very Spanish inasmuch as it captures all the average contemporary ideas and prejudices of Spain in politics, morals, and religion. It also succeeds in pointing up the color and romance of the country in a series of highly evocative images, scenes and characters.

The contrary thesis to this is that Cervantes was steeped, through wide and deep reading, in the liberal thinking which was prevalent in 16th-Century Europe. It has been suggested in this connection that he came under the influence of Erasmism to a much greater extent than appears at first. He had therefore developed ideas on such topics as nationalism and the Church which were far advanced of his contemporaries. His thought embraces a unity which is revealed in his novel, and he must be considered among Spain's most extraordinary intellectual writers. He can be regarded as a child of the Counter-reformation, and the liberal beliefs he espoused are hidden beneath ironical allusions which must not be taken in the literal sense. For this reason he was forced into a position of what has been described as righteous hypocrisy.

2. What argument is there against Lord Byron's idea that this satire on Spanish ideals constitutes treason?

ANSWER: Cervantes has been accused of almost personally sponsoring Spanish decadence by writing *Don Quixote*. His purpose, however, was not to shatter any noble ideals, but rather just the opposite—to purify them and help discard some of the more unsavory elements which might taint these ideals. Cervantes aimed to purify and salvage the chivalric ideal, and therein lies the true meaning of his novel—although Cervantes was probably unaware of this as he was writing it. Regarding the work merely as a satire limits the novel's scope and restricts the reader's vision. When we regard the book in its widest sense, it takes on social, historical, and national dimensions much wider than those we get on a purely satirical level. The most important feature of 16th- and 17th-Century Spanish politics, both internal and external, was the myopic attitude of a nation enraptured with the idea of its own grandeur. This led, of course, to an unwillingness to realize that the world was changing, and to a reverence for outworn ideas. In this attitude lies potential disaster. Yet there was an absurd contrast in the social milieu in which Cervantes was writing: there were grave national weaknesses and overweening ambitions; there was a vacuity of intellectual thinking couched in a pompous, inflated language; and there was grinding poverty placed in a gorgeous "stage-setting" atmosphere. Don Quixote chases phantoms which exist only in his febrile imagination, and in so doing is battling for some vague form of universal unity—everywhere he goes, for example, he attempts to make everyone he meets extol the sovereign beauty of Dulcinea. Yet there is a bitter lesson to be learned at every turn. One does not have to work tremendously hard to find this philosophy in the novel, and it goes far out beyond the bounds of plain satire. In the long run, the best argument against Byron's thesis is the fact of the book's essential humanity and accessibility to all types of audience. Its moral and philosophy are detectable, but cannot be pinned down to any one school of thought; it is universally human. *Don Quixote* is a book in which the qualities of optimism are extolled, a book into which we can look to find life, not just a theory *about* life.

3. Discuss the mingling of realism and romantic tales in Cervantes' novel.

ANSWER: Critics have often attacked Cervantes for the manner in which he allowed romantic tales to intrude on the realistic aspects of his story. To begin with, the realistic aspects of the story are provided by the everyday adventures which Don Quixote and Sancho Panza encounter on the road. Yet the whole point of the story is that Don Quixote's ludicrous pretensions will be highlighted by the commonplace realism of these adventures. Nevertheless, it is true that the story-telling introduced into the first part of the book is out of place and not quite in keeping with the general tone of the whole work. There are two possible reasons for the use of these stories. The first is that Cervantes was giving way to his natural tendency toward story-telling, and the second is that he did not wish the list of everyday adventures to become monotonous. It must be admitted, however, that the first part of the book is spoiled to a great extent by such unevenness, and the whole work could undoubtedly be improved by a more unifying effect on the variety of tales and incidents. There is an overall lack of cohesion, plot and character development throughout the book, and, as George Santayana has pointed out, there is throughout a strong element of improvisation. The incidents and stories seem to have been written on the spur of the moment, with little thought of their place in the general framework of the tale. The success of the book considered as a story depends, therefore, on the ingenuity and efficacy of each story and incident as it takes place. Its narrative elements must be judged on the intrinsic, spasmodic effects they contain, and on the brilliance of the characterization. It is tempting, of course, to totally denigrate this mode of writing fiction. Yet on the positive side, it is an exciting and fanciful technique, depending for its success on graphic descriptive ability and ingenuity of style. When we take these requisites into consideration, Don Quixote is a masterpiece in its own right. Furthermore, the style of the work is facile and flowing, colored by varieties of background for the discourses and adventures of Sancho and Don Quixote. So in a very special way, the book is unified when we take all these qualities into consideration, and it takes its permanent place among the world's great works because of the very combination of all these elements—including, of course, the element of rollicking humor, with which it abounds.

4. G. K. Chesterton once described Don Quixote as a "Divine Parody." How would you regard this viewpoint?

ANSWER: To begin with, we must remember that Chesterton was a great champion of medievalism and viewed the Middle Ages through the eyes of a chivalric romanticist. Bearing this in mind, we should judge his description of *Don Quixote* with a certain degree of critical suspicion, while granting the fact that he does present a thought-provoking point of view. What, then, was Chesterton's point? He regarded as quite superfluous any learned or academic approach to Cervantes' book, and went further by claiming that literature exists to celebrate the eternity of youth. On this point alone he can be easily attacked, although he is correct in claiming that *Don Quixote* can be read by a child for its story alone, without any reference to symbolism or profound interpretation. This does not mean to say, however, that there is no symbolic profundity in the book, and Chesterton is unwilling to look behind the story itself. He questions Goethe's claim that the first part is superior to the second because of the ludicrous picturesqueness which makes the tournament of windmills so vivid. Chesterton agrees that the first part *is* in fact superior, but it is so because it contains the fire of medieval romance and spiritual energy. The conflict in the story is not between idealism and realism as opposing factors, but between the Knight's mysticism and the Squire's rationalism, both of which are parts of the same good. If there *is* anything behind the story, it is an element of divine irony, one which tells us that we inhabit an infuriatingly perplexing world in which *we are all correct*. Chesterton is himself showing a romantic idealism here which is one of his major flaws as a thinker. He sees *Don Quixote* as a work which merely proclaims the wholesomely divine message that man is basically good. Cervantes is praised for displaying to humanity the fundamental truth that lawlessness is merely an eternal battle between a hundred justices. The character of Don Quixote himself appeals to us because we all have the mad elements of his nature in our blood, and we are all offsprings of the Middle Ages. We are knights-errant at heart, according to Chesterton, tilting our lances at the great windmill of life, and therein lies the universal appeal of Cervantes' work. While we may find this interpretation of *Don Quixote* exciting and stimulating in a romantic kind of way, we should beware of Chesterton's tendency to simplify such works by reducing them to terms of robust romanticism and a kind of merry medieval mysticism.

5. Discuss the use of the contrasting and paradoxical aspects of *Don Quixote*.

ANSWER: It is interesting to note that the conversations between the two main characters do not serve to further the plot, but rather concentrate on the mighty theme of knight-errantry. As we read the book, we are aware of the great store of rational arguments with which Don Quixote defends his fluctuating faith, and we cannot help observing the effect which these rationalizations have on Sancho. This process, of course, ends with the knight's deterioration of belief in himself, which leads in turn to his death, when he is restored to the bleak domain of sanity. It can really be regarded paradoxically as retrogressive progress from the richness of absolute faith to the utter poverty of skepticism. Throughout the whole work, this atmosphere of contrasting tensions is maintained, first in the complex character of the knight, and secondly in the attitudes of his squire. There is, for example, the conflict between situations as they really are and how they appear to Don Quixote; there is the marked contrast between the knight's inflated, aristocratic postures and his squire's peasant-like insights; and, of course, there is always the tension between the hero's rational sanity on the one hand and his irrational fantasies on the subject of chivalry. Each incident in the book contains the nucleus of at least one of these contrasting tensions. This leads in turn to a stylistic contrast in the book, inasmuch as the loosely strung events *do* have a cohesion when we concentrate on each incident, bearing in mind the fact that each one contains a conflict. There is also a strong element of linguistic contrast running throughout the book. Don Quixote's madness has its own level of inflated rhetoric and pompous imagery which, combined with the majestic irony of his speeches, stands in marked contrast to the plain, idiomatic language of everyday talk. In a very real sense, of course, the self-contradictory hub of the novel is Don Quixote's madness, which can be regarded as quite simply madness, but which takes on much wider dimensions when we realize that it opens up to us the whole problem of Truth. When we ask ourselves why he *was* mad, the answer is that he actually believed that the books of medieval, romantic Chivalry were, in fact, quite literally true. In those days, many people probably *did* believe that true history was being recorded in these romances. What *made* Don Quixote mad was that he tried to translate them into action. Yet by the same token, we could point the same finger of accusation at religious hermits who attempt to achieve spiritual perfection by imitating the early Desert Fathers. The whole issue is really brought to a head in the conflict between Don Quixote and the innkeeper, who believes that the books on knight-errantry were true, but that they had lapsed into antiquity merely because he himself had never experienced the chivalric tradition. In this context, therefore, one cannot really say that Don Quixote was mad and the innkeeper was sane, and leave it at that. What caused the conflict was what we can call the tension of opposing perspectives on moral, experiental, and historical levels. Don Quixote wants to play his heroic role in history by doing good deeds in the true chivalric tradition, while the innkeeper is happy to regard such conduct as belonging to past history—to him, the world exists as something to be cheated, not saved. We can quite safely say that when regarded in this light, madness can be linked to nobility of character in the knight, and sanity to the banal standards of the innkeeper.

The conflict between belief and disbelief can also be seen in Sancho Panza's attitudes. When he believes, he does so because he is influenced by Don Quixote's grandiloquence and by his own intrinsic greed. His doubts, however, are based on the fact that he does not have his master's sense of lofty purpose nor his bookish knowledge. It is important to remember, too, that the more esoteric aspects of these romantic books were in fact believed, on the whole, and that in this historical context it is unfair to dismiss Don Quixote as nothing but a mad, gullible dupe. He indeed leads a life based on delusion, but it is delusion with a noble purpose, namely to rise above the torpid monotony of daily existence and perform noble deeds. In this respect, the knight is the most admirable character in the book—and he also happens to be the most intelligent. This intelligence is, of course, brought out often in oblique and paradoxical ways, for Don Quixote's dialectic becomes positively brilliant when he has a hopeless position to defend.

6. How would you describe the purpose behind the writing of Don Quixote?

ANSWER: One can start off by accepting the dictum that Cervantes was first and foremost a humorist, someone who found more value in a funny story or in an amusing incident than he did in any moral values or in such these as religion, the chivalric tradition, or patriotism. If this is the case, Cervantes is in fact a great iconoclast, helping to break down centuries of national tradition by a process of studied mockery. *Don Quixote* can also be regarded, for the same reasons, as a great tragedy —a point of view held by the great English critic, John Ruskin. This point of view is reached ultimately if we accept the fact that the knight was totally defeated in his idealism, in his dreams of defending ladies in distress and helping the poor. But was Don Quixote a failure? In the narrowest sense, he was indeed a ludicrous and absurd failure. Yet in the widest sense, he triumphs over all who tackle him, from innkeeper, barber, student, or silk merchant, because Cervantes maintains and sponsors throughout the work a rare sense of values. This brings us to the problem of the purpose behind the writing of the book, and for an answer to this we must first examine what Cervantes himself thought of the matter.

To begin with, Cervantes considered that there were too few entertaining books around, and wanted quite simply to write one. Coupled with this, of course, was the conscious aim of attacking the vogue of chivalric literature, with its tradition of high romance and marvelous improbability. He also intended it to be a simple tale. Let us point out from the outset that Cervantes succeeded in these purposes, but also succeeded in doing much more than he intended. He brings the traditional romantic hero down to earth, making him natural and human to the extent that the knight's lofty ideals are shattered because of the futility of overwhelming the external conditions of everyday life. While Don Quixote is fascinated with the chivalric tradition of doing good, he is ignorant of its practical application—he liberates Andrew, for example, and leaves him unprotected. In this respect, *Don Quixote* is an attack on utopian idealism and stands as an attack on the starry-eyed reformers whose plans to reform the world inevitably end up in disaster. World reformers ride along on the Rocinantes of their dreams, attacking the windmills of tradition with no regard for the depths and strength of their foundations. Yet we must bear in mind that Cervantes is not passing critical judgement on the excellence of idealistic motivation, but on the futility and absurdity of the attempt. In *Don Quixote* there is also an inherent admiration for the refusal on the part of the utopians to surrender to despair—note how the knight, for example, will not retire to his village. Cervantes is not really critical of his hero for his sense of humanitarian and chivalric idealism, but rather for the absurd self-deification which accompanies such a posture. In one way, it is a sad and bitter work inasmuch as Cervantes is making the devastatingly ironical comment that there is no place for saint, philanthropist or philosopher on a universal scale. There is a Spanish saying that Christ asks each man to bear his own cross, but not that of his neighbor. *Don Quixote* set out to defy this precept, and ended up dying before his time. Yet this is exactly where the puzzling paradox of the book comes in. For while the hero's attempt to attain the impossible makes the work one of disillusion and despair, seen from one angle, it is a work of stimulating optimism when viewed from another. In Don Quixote's failure dwells the triumph of the human spirit over the gross impersonalities of life which try to stifle it, and in this way the book is a permanent tribute to man's indomitable will, power of perseverance, and stoical strength in the face of apparently insurmountable social obstacles. Lord Byron once said that in *Don Quixote*, Cervantes "smiled Spain's chivalry away." This is a fair surface appraisal of the book's purpose, but when we look beneath the surface we find that Cervantes is really smiling away the external and impersonal modes of time-honored traditions. He is also attacking the lack of inner conviction which manifests itself in the misuse of religion, absence of social justice, and abuse of external power. The hero, for all his external absurdities, stands as a tribute to inner individualism crushed and killed by the impersonal, but not destroyed, inasmuch as his spirit represents that mysterious ability of man to defy to the end the titanic forces which he can never defeat.

7. Ivan Turgenev wrote a famous essay contrasting what Don Quixote represents with what Hamlet represents. How would you summarize and appraise his point of view?

ANSWER: Turgenev took the point of view that these two great literary figures represent the opposite poles of man's nature, and that all men embody the qualities of either Don Quixote or of Hamlet. One set of men live according to a code of ideals which lies outside themselves, and spend their lives attempting to fit their actions into this external mold. The other type continually submits this external ideal to his own personal value judgements. Turgenev tries to prove that these two human attitudes are embodied in Cervantes' knight and Shakespeare's prince, and does so by outlining what each character represents. First of all, the Russian dismisses the view that Don Quixote is merely "the Knight of the sorrowful figure," drawn to lampoon chivalric romances. The knight represents to Turgenev faith in some external truth which *can* be achieved by an all-consuming personal devotion and self-abnegation. Don Quixote is willing to sacrifice himself for this ideal, for such self-immolation will mean the establishment of truth and justice on earth. Admittedly, there is an absurdity in the fantasy involved, but nevertheless the knight lives "outside himself," dedicated to the abolition of all forces hostile to man's well-being. He is the antithesis of the egotistical hero, totally devoted to self-sacrifice. He is not plagued with self-doubt, and is fully aware of his purpose in life. Despite his madness—and to him the wooden puppets really *are* Moors—there is a dignity to his judgements. Don Quixote is the slave of an ideal.

What does Hamlet represent, on the other hand? He is a supreme egotist, living entirely for himself. He cannot find anything outside himself on which he can pin his values. Hamlet is a sceptic, doubting everything, even that which he finds within himself. He is conscious of his own weakness, wallowing in self-deprecation. This is in violent contrast to Don Quixote's boundless enthusiasm. Yet there is a vainglorious nourishment in Hamlet's introspection which prevents him from committing suicide, and a love of life shows through his very contemplation of death. Hamlet suffers, and his suffering is much more painful and frustrating than that of Don Quixote's. The knight is battered by shepherds and convicts, while Hamlet pummels himself with the cudgel of self-analysis. Don Quixote shows a deep respect for the existing order, such as religion and the monarchy, while Hamlet is scornful of royalty and priests. Cervantes' character has definite ideas on such matters as government, while Hamlet has no time or desire to think of such things. Turgenev concludes his comparison by stating that Don Quixote represents discovery and Hamlet symbolizes development, and that they are both archetypal figures set poles apart, the enthusiasm of the one lending itself to comedy and the introspection of the other leading to tragedy. He also points out that in real life, it is seldom that one encounters the purely comic and the purely tragic, and that life tends toward these positions but never reaches them.

Very briefly, Turgenev's summing up of Don Quixote's position is too definitive, and ignores the complexities of his character. It is true that he does indulge in an eternal chase after an externalized ideal, but this does not negate the possibility of his having an inner position which he sustains. It could be argued that Don Quixote *is* the supreme egotist of literature, pitting his overweening ego against the windmills of impersonal forces. Again, it could well be claimed that Hamlet's position is totally dominated by an external ideal, and that he is a *non*-egotistical figure in that his "self" has been engulfed by forces too huge for him to cope with. Again, Hamlet is certainly scornful of kings and priests; but then, he was a prince and could afford to show such defiance. Even then, Turgenev's argument that Don Quixote bowed to the existing order could be questioned. In many ways, his expedition is a one-man crusade against the organization of the social, religious, and political order. Quite generally. Turgenev can be taken to task for having placed Don Quixote and Hamlet into categories too neatly parcelled for such complex, puzzling, and dynamic personalities.

8. Discuss the relationship between Don Quixote and Sancho Panza with particular reference to their contrasting qualities.

ANSWER: These two contrasting characters stand at the very core of the novel, and their relationship is highlighted by the conversations held between them. On one level, they represent two clear-cut positions: the knight stands for altruism, bookish wisdom and madness, and his squire symbolizes selfishness, earthy intelligence, and sanity. Yet the contrast is not quite as clear-cut as that, since they affect each other's position as the book progresses to such an extent that we eventually get what the Spanish critic Madariaga called the "sanchification of Don Quixote and the quixotification of Sancho." In one sense, they are both driven by external ideals—the knight by dreams of chivalric glory and the squire for hopes of worldly wealth. This process of continual argument and counter-argument continues until the servant feels at times the peer of the master. This results at times in the Don's becoming jealous. When Sancho finds the delights of glory in the chivalric sense, for example, or Don Quixote becomes childishly envious at Sancho's receiving the island, the foibles of human nature are being exposed in the simplest and most delightful terms. It should be remembered that although the knight's peculiar brand of insanity causes him to see everything in terms of medieval romance, he does talk with a nobility which makes him grow in stature. And as he grows, his page grows correspondingly. In modern dramatic terms, Sancho can be described as a comic foil who grows wiser in one way as the leading man grows wiser in another. In the widest human terms, they grow to represent two genres of human wisdom, the one recognizing life as it is and the other appreciating life as it ought to be. Sancho's type of wisdom gives him an immediate sense of how to deal practically with a given situation, while the Don is so enraptured with dreams of chivalric glory that he deals with a crisis according to the idealistic norm of romantic virtue.

Take, for example, the scene in which Don Quixote advances through the wood, prepared to encounter the giants who are making such a dreadful din. When it is discovered that the fulling-hammers of a mill are causing the sound, Sancho laughs at him. Now how are we to judge the two characters by their reaction to this scene? We can say that the knight is totally irrational and insane, and that the squire is a sane, rational human being. In a practical sense this is true, but should we judge the merits of a great literary character by his practical qualities? Don Quixote, within the context of his world of fantasy, displays an inner readiness and an outer courage to face the giants, who are as real to him as they are imaginary to Sancho. We must remember that in each one of these adventures, the Don and his page are both right and wrong. The knight fails in each one of his encounters, but he is never inconsistent. He wears the fantastic emblem of chivalric honor with pride to the very end. At some point in the story the reader must pause and ask himself where the demarcation line is between imaginative fantasy and complete insanity. Couched in its widest terms, the problem is this: to what extent does humanity in general or the artist in particular choose to remain a Sancho while giving rein to the Don Quixote within him? In a very immediate way, Cervantes himself was faced with that very dilemma. He found himself in the position of the Renaissance figure caught between the necessities of practical life and the impulses of an idealistic temperament; between Aristotelianism and Platonism; between logical realism and romantic poetry; in short, between the Sancho and the Don Quixote of his own nature.

Much of the book is taken up with a long, almost ceremonially bizarre dialogue between the two characters which assumes various dimensions of meaning and proportions of intensity. This has the effect of helping to unify what at first glance appears to be a long string of unrelated incidents, because once an episode takes place, it crops up again in the argument of one of the two protagonists. A good example of this reminiscent technique is the way Don Quixote continually recalls the blanket-tossing incident—in which, it will be remembered, he had failed to rescue Sancho, blaming the episode on the work of enchanters—every time the topic of enchantment comes up in conversation. In short, no one event is finished with completely once it is over. Technically, this is a very clever and very subtle fictional device for which Cervantes has not been given full credit. The mnemonic effect of these recurring episodes is of great importance to this novel psychologically and effectually. The critic Gerald Brenan very cleverly compares the relationship between the two to that of a married couple. If we regard the Don as playing the role of the unmitigated male, and Sancho as being the half-dependent female who is gradually gaining ascendancy in the relationship, much of the second part of the book makes greater sense. Sancho finally achieves a kind of ludicrous dominance over his failing master, and, when the Don dies sane yet unfulfilled, he at least leaves Sancho behind to continue in the absurd capacity of an inflated, preposterously prosperous male widowhood.

It must also be noted that through the development of the knight and the squire, and their relations with outside events and other people, a subtle dramatic unity is sustained which

Cervantes himself admitted he found almost intolerable. The whole array of characters—duchesses, damsels in distress, innkeepers, and so on—are introduced more or less to play upon the two central figures, to make them act, interact, and react. The resultant dialogues on the nature of reality and the various ways in which the two characters respond to their respective views of reality are of paramount importance, of course. Yet we should never approach *Don Quixote* as we do a quasi-philosophical treatise. We should rather view it as a panoramic view of humanity with its follies, doubts, delusions, greeds and flashes of sagacity. These universal characteristics are all embodied in the individual characters of the Don and his page, and are heightened by the gallery of characters whom they encounter on the way. And therein lies the immediate and ultimate wisdom of this book. Although Cervantes undoubtedly did not intend it, he gave his work a permanence by his power of suggesting, in every scene between the knight and the squire, very much more than what is actually said or performed.

9. Discuss Don Quixote from the point of view of plot, construction, style, and Cervantes' place in the history of chivalric literature.

ANSWER: Cervantes was well acquainted with the works of chivalric literature which preceded him. It must not be thought, however, that his attitude to them was in any way one of contempt. On the contrary, he admired the qualities which they promoted, namely generosity of spirit, noble idealism, courage, single-mindedness of purpose, and loyalty. Nevertheless, Cervantes did find fault with the world of romance when it clashed with the world of reality. *Don Quixote* is in this respect the turning point of romantic literature, and it is absolutely erroneous to regard it as the last of the great medieval romances. In many respects it heralds a new era in literature, since it combines the best of romantic fiction and the picaresque form of novel. In blending the real with the unreal, in fusing the romantic with the mundane, in contrasting the idealistic with the practical, Cervantes created something quite revolutionary in the history of literature. It is interesting to note, in the history of Cervantes' personal development as a writer, that his first book, the *Galatea,* embraced all the pastoral elements of the older type of novel, and that his last work, the *Travails of Persiles and Sigismunda,* in many ways is also in the tradition of medieval romantic literature. Fortunately, however, he was also well acquainted with the picaresque novel, which dealt with the life of the slums and with the character of vagabonds, thieves and rogues of all descriptions. Cervantes' collected stories, the *Novelas Ejemplares,* make interesting reading, not only as examples of this picaresque form of fiction, but also as evidence of preparation for his masterpiece, *Don Quixote.* We must therefore bear in mind the fact that Cervantes was drawing on two literary modes, the romantic and the picaresque, when he wrote his great work.

It is almost certain that Cervantes started writing *Don Quixote* with some of the episodes clearly worked out in advance. He probably planned to have the crazy knight undergo some adventures in the early chapters, followed by the examination and burning of the offensive books, and ending with his restoration to the world of sanity. It is generally considered that the character of Sancho Panza was an afterthought, but in any case, the initial idea was extended to a book consisting of four parts, which we now refer to as Part I, published in 1605. It was by its very conception a loosely constructed book, but, as we have pointed out, the nature of the work did not demand a tightly knit and compact form. As a deliberate attempt to prevent the novel's becoming a tedious dialogue between the Don and Sancho, Cervantes introduced much variety of character, incident, and scenery. In so doing, of course, he almost unwittingly added to the tremendously symbolic impact of the whole work as embodied in the two central figures. For this reason, we find that *Don Quixote* in some ways embraces every kind of contemporary fiction. The chapter about the galley-slaves, for example, is picaresque; the pastoral tradition is found in the story of Marcela and Chrysostom; while the tale of the captive is a miniature adventure novel. Cervantes came under some criticism for this interweaving of short stories into the main fabric of Part I, and for that reason practically abandoned it altogether when he came to write Part II.

It is almost impossible to classify Cervantes' style, since he employed several styles to suit the mood and theme of his narration. A great deal of *Don Quixote,* however, is written in that facile, earthy, racy style which the Spanish call *estilo llano.* But when he comes to the parts in which he is parodying the turgid, stilted verbiage of the traditional romances, he switches to platitudes and archaisms. In the story of the captive, he employs a plain, simple style. The passage on the Golden Age is embellished with the rhetorical polish of his earlier works. It is unfortunate that the care with which Cervantes altered his style is not fully appreciated, to the extent that he is often accused of being an extremely slovenly and uneven writer stylistically.

10. Why is the adventure of Montesinos' Cave often held up as one of the highlights of *Don Quixote?*

ANSWER: This particular passage in the novel is a superb example of Cervantes ability to evoke subtle effects by an almost uncanny power of suggestion. It should be made clear that it is not merely another mock-heroic incident, but has in fact much wider dimensions. Cervantes has done something here that suggests a touch of genius: he has taken a part of the Grail legend, and, without losing any of the haunting beauty, poetic mysticism, and unsentimental reverence surrounding the legend, he has reduced it to human proportions and made it absurd. What is even more remarkable is the fact that Cervantes has achieved this feat by a series of deft touches by Don Quixote himself. One interpretation of this is that Cervantes is making the knight mouth his (the author's) own brand of satire, while parodying his (Don Quixote's) own character. This in itself would be a clever literary device, and would be a satisfactory explanation of the scene's success, were it not for the fact that Cervantes makes it quite clear that what we have here is Don Quixote's vision. In this respect, it should be noted that an atmosphere of dream and fantasy shrouds the entire passage, adding a uniquely subtle and strangely beautiful flavor to the absurdity of it all. And throughout it, a new aspect of Don Quixote's character comes through. There is nothing remarkable, of course, about the castle or the fact that Montesinos is enchanted and gives a speech of welcome. These are all aspects of the knight's world of fantasy, and we are, therefore, prepared for them. What seems out of place, however, and what *does* surprise us is the remarkable degree of realism the scene contains. The references to the weight of the heart and to Belerma's skin, for example, have a dual effect. They translate us from the world of romance to the world of reality, but more important, they reveal a basic, prosaic, mundane quality in Don Quixote, who has set himself up as the knight-errant on a one-man mission against a prosaic and mundane world. Set in the atmosphere of one of the knight's own dreams, this is a brilliant piece of characterization by Cervantes.

Added to this, of course, we have the disturbingly cynical remarks of Durandarte expressing doubt as to the knight's ability to free him from his enchantment. There is also the scene in which Dulcinea's maid asks for a small loan, but there is a subtle insinuation behind the ostensible inappropriateness of this request. Apparently the ladies of Spain's fashionable world were accustomed to asking for loans from elderly men who were, by implication, absurd parodies of knights-errant, as is Don Quixote. The request is, therefore, a brilliantly subtle touch on the part of Cervantes. For the author himself is satirizing the ludicrous aspects of the relationships between young, hard-headed women and elderly, foolish gallants. A voice within Don Quixote himself is telling him, within his dream, that if any lady responds to his advances, it will be for money only. There is, therefore, an uncommon touch of poignancy and depth of insight in what appears to be totally inconsequential remark.

In modern terms, this dream gives us a glimpse into one of the dark recesses of Don Quixote's subconscious mind. It is tremendously important in any appraisal of the knight's character, for it shows that Don Quixote, even in his private, triumphant world of fantasy dreamed up in the safe world of sleep, is never free from the gnawing truths of the real world. It is almost as if the world of illusion and fantasy, no matter how apparently all-embracing, is always vulnerable, always a prey to attack by the bitter truths of reality.

11. How would you appraise Cervantes and his novel in the context of 17th-Century thought and literature?

ANSWER: A thorough appraisal of Cervantes and his novel is impossible without some background in the literary sensibility and intellectual climate of the age in which he lived. Cervantes grew up in an atmosphere of what the Spanish call *gracia,* which can best be described as a kind of humorous, disinterested attitude to the passing scene, tempered with native wisdom, subtlety, and a sense of the absurd. And when an author captured all the elements of a scene which satisfied his artistic sense, he wrote with what is called *discreción,* which is a type of dry, subtle, and ironic wit. These influences obviously had an effect on Cervantes as a writer, but his major work is also affected by an atmosphere of disillusion, and our knowledge of his life and temperament shows us how much this played on his character. Furthermore, this novel is written very much in the Renaissance humanistic spirit of the supremacy of Reason and down-to-earth morality. The dogma of Original Sin, which had burst forth into Spanish theology through the influence of Calvinists and Lutherans, is absent from the works of Cervantes. He retained a thoroughly liberal spirit which, paradoxically enough, made his works seem stilted and rather antiquated to many of his contemporaries. Cervantes was educated, of course, in the Erasmist tradition, which also helps to lend his great work that special touch of universality which has made its survival possible. It is interesting to note that his works were first recognized for their greatness outside Spain. Nevertheless, it should be pointed out that *Don Quixote,* while humanistic in the best Renaissance sense, is not entirely free from the 17th-Century tendencies toward hagiography, epistemological debates, and theological complexities. While Cervantes owed much to the past, he was still susceptible to the influences of the present.

The European novel as an art form owes a great debt to Cervantes. Such eminent English authors as Henry Fielding and Tobias Smollett admitted having learned a great deal from him. Much also may be said of *Don Quixote* on a metaphysical level of appraisal, for it contains many more profundities than it has often been credited with. It should be pointed out, of course, that Cervantes did not set out to write a profoundly metaphysical book. Yet the same could undoubtedly be said of Shakespeare or Dostoevsky in relation to some of their greatest works. Accepting the fact of there being a metaphysical aspect to *Don Quixote,* how can we interpret it cogently? Put in its simplest terms, it might be said that the book represents an absurd tension between man's innate need for a faith, and his ability to grasp one due to intellectual disillusion. Don Quixote, who has an intellect, loses his illusion and dies. Sancho Panza, the non-intellectual, survives and flourishes. It has been said of *Don Quixote* that it was written with the pen of doubt upon the paper of conviction. Probably its greatest virtue is its undeniable sense of humanity, despite its obvious, faults, which include crudities in places and occasional tedium. It is the type of work to which the reader has to bring a great deal in order to receive insights which the book warrants.

12. What indications does the book give us of contemporary Spanish life?

ANSWER: *Don Quixote* gives a sweeping picture of Spanish customs, way of life, and social strata. A great deal of the action, of course, takes place along the roads and in the inns of the country, and almost every type of person and profession is brought in front of us. Even though a few incidents occur in remote places, we are always acutely aware of the grandeur of the Spanish background, which lends color and vitality to the action. Socially, every type is represented. The picaresque aspects of the book give us a view of the underworld in the conversations of the chain-gang convicts. Skilled workers also have their place in the portrait of the bookmaker and printer in Barcelona. The higher level of society is represented by the Duke and Duchess and by Don Ferdinand's father, all of whom live in resplendent luxury. We are also made aware of the awe in which the upper classes were held by those in an inferior position. The middle classes are personified by the judge, and by the lady going to join her husband in Seville. The influence which the earlier Spanish pastoral romances had on Cervantes also comes through in his portraits of shepherds and shepherdesses, but it must be admitted that these are the most unrealistic personality descriptions in the book.

Don Quixote has been described as an allegory of the Spanish character and temperament, and this is particularly true when

we consider the character of Don Quixote himself. He is in
many ways a totally non-compromising character, and this element of rigid inflexibility is a feature attributed to the Spanish
make-up. His opinions are held almost as a way of challenging
other people, an attitude very closely linked to the Spanish
conception of honor. Don Quixote displays his sense of honor
like a chivalric emblem, something to be inordinately proud of
and something worth fighting for to the death. There is, of
course, an element of fanaticism in this, but it is a fanaticism
brought out only when this sense of honor is challenged. Don
Quixote, even in his most absurd moments, shows this trait,
but he also shows the other Spanish traits of tolerance, a feeling
for humanity, and uncommon kindness. All this, of course,
makes *Don Quixote* an outstanding work. It has elements of
universality and individual characterization brilliantly executed,
while the variegated aspects of everyday Spanish life, far from
being neglected, serve to intensify the dramatic, moral and
psychological aspects of its contents.

CRITICAL COMMENTARY

LORD BYRON (19th Century):   Lord Byron said of Cervantes that "he smil'd the chivalry of Spain away."

GUSTAVE FLAUBERT (19th Century):   Flaubert said, "I find my own origins in that book which I knew by heart before I knew how to read."

ANATOLE FRANCE (19th Century):   In *Le livre de mon ami,* France said, "Woe to him who is not sometimes a Don Quixote, and who never took windmills for giants! This great-souled Don Quixote was his own enchanter. He put nature on an equality with his own soul. That is not being duped! The dupes are they who see before them nothing beautiful or great!"

WILLIAM HAZLITT (19th Century):   Hazlitt said, "The character of Don Quixote himself is one of the most perfect disinterestedness. He is an enthusiast of the most amiable kind; of a nature equally open, gentle, and generous; a lover of truth and justice; and one who had brooded over fine dreams of chivalry and romance, till they had robbed him of himself, and cheated his brain into a belief of their reality.

"There cannot be a greater mistake than to consider *Don Quixote* as a merely satirical work, or as a vulgar attempt to explode 'the long-forgotten order of chivalry'. There could be no need to explode what no longer existed. Besides, Cervantes himself was a man of the most sanguine and enthusiastic temperament, and even through the carved and battered figure of the knight the spirit of chivalry shines out with undiminished lustre; as if the author had half-designed to revive the example of past ages, and once more 'witch the world with noble horsemanship'."

JOHN RUSKIN (19th Century):   Ruskin said of Cervantes' novel, *"Don Quixote* always affected me throughout to tears, not laughter. It was always throughout real chivalry to me: it is precisely because the most touching valor and tenderness were rendered vain by madness . . . and because all true chivalry is thus by implication accused of madness and involved in shame that I call the book so deadly."

IVAN TURGENEV (19th Century):   In his essay called *Hamlet and Don Quixote,* Turgenev says, "The Don Quixotes discover; the Hamlets develop. But how, I shall be asked, can the Hamlets evolve anything when they doubt all things and believe in nothing? My rejoinder is that, by a wise dispensation of Nature, there are neither thorough Hamlets nor complete Don Quixotes; these are but extreme manifestations of two tendencies—guide-posts set up by the poets on two different roads. Life tends toward them, but never reaches the goal. We must not forget that, just as the principle of analysis is carried in Hamlet to tragedy, so the element of enthusiasm runs in Don Quixote to comedy; but in life, the purely comic and the purely tragic are seldom encountered."

ROBERT M. ADAMS (20th Century):   In his *Strains of Discord,* Adams says that *Don Quixote* can be read on two levels. The first is that on which the hero is seen as a Christian figure, setting forth on a personal mission to salvage the world. Although his pilgrimage is strewn with earthly battles, these are justified as the means toward the ultimate goal of heavenly peace. He adopts a consistently Christian attitude as the novel progresses, and his conversations center more and more on theological matters, to such an extent that Sancho Panzo is forced to comment on them. The second level is that on which Don Quixote is a buffoon, mocked, beaten, and blundering through everything. Far from a kind of pilgrim's progress, the novel can be viewed as a slapstick comedy. This dual nature of the book creates a dilemma for the reader, since its total impact is not unified.

GERALD BRENAN (20th Century):   In his *Literature of the Spanish People,* Brenan deplores the fact that *Don Quixote* is largely neglected as a novel in the present century. He says the reason for this neglect lies in the fact that our opinion of the book is still very much influenced by the simplified interpretations given to it by Victorian critics. Brenan says that the subject of the book is really militant and revolutionary faith, and that the psychology of belief and half-belief is explained by Cervantes as it has never been done before or since. Yet while Cervantes has made the hero of his book a revolutionary figure, he still casts doubts on Don Quixote's motives. Emotionally, Cervantes gives us the impression that he is on the side of his hero, but nevertheless censures him. For all his flaws, however, Don Quixote is the one great and noble figure in the book.

AMERICA CASTRO (20th Century): In *El pensamiento de Cervantes,* Castro says that Cervantes, being deeply read in the liberal writings of the 16th Century, came under the influence of Erasmism to a much greater extent than has been imagined. As a result, he had extremely advanced views on such contemporary aspects of Spanish life as nationalism, the Moriscos, and the Church. For this reason, he holds an honored position among the enlightened and aristocratic thinkers of Spanish literary history. Castro goes on to claim that the Counter-Reformation quite literally forced Cervantes to conceal his true meanings behind veiled ironies and allusions, which most readers erroneously take in their literal sense. Critics of Castro's theory claim that he failed to distinguish between Cervantes and his characters.

G. K. CHESTERTON (20th Century): In *A Handful of Authors,* Chesterton says that the most important feature of *Don Quixote* lies in the fact that it embraces a conflict of goods. To illustrate his point, he cites the battle between the idealism of Don Quixote and the realism of the innkeeper, claiming that the struggle is so intense and apparently unending that both of the positions represented must be right. Chesterton expands his thesis by claiming that the book is not a jeremiad bewailing the evil of the world, but rather that it points out one of life's ultimate truths: namely, that much of the bewildering turmoil of the world is caused by the clash and conflict of so many good philosophies.

JOHN DRINKWATER (20th Century): In *The Outline of Literature,* Drinkwater says that Cervantes is totally a Renaissance figure. He wrote in a 16th-Century atmosphere of national glory, and the critic claims that, apart from the plays of Shakespeare, *Don Quixote* is the greatest and most beautiful product of Renaissance literature. He proceeds with the idea that although Cervantes started writing the book with the idea of attacking the whole conception of chivalry, which had become rather ludicrous by the 16th Century, the more universal and allegorical aspects of the work grew organically during the process of its composition.

FITZMAURICE-KELLY (20th Century): He said that Cervantes' presentation of all strata of society, from nobles, knights, accomplished ladies and courtly gentlemen, to simple country girls, traders, poets, priests, and farmers, is made with sympathy of insight. He further says that its immediate success was due to the colorful variety of its scenes and incidents, and also to the obvious thrusts which Cervantes is making at well-known contemporary figures. Other aspects of the novel, such as its deep analysis of life, its sense of humanity, and its pathos, took more time to be appreciated.

FORD MADOX FORD (20th Century): Mr. Ford takes a very disparaging view of Cervantes' novel in his critical work, *The March of Literature*. He even goes so far as to say that the world has been done a great disservice by its very existence. Ford's thesis is that the idea of chivalry, which Cervantes was ridiculing in his book, might have been able to save our civilization from disaster. The critic goes on to accuse Cervantes of vulgarity in encouraging puerile minds to mock the catastrophes of the knight of La Mancha. Ford then expresses amazement that someone like Cervantes, whom he attacks as a fraud and a hack writer, could even have thought up such a beautiful figure as Don Quixote. He calls the work a "Masterpiece of ill taste," and claims that it merely succeeded in leaving the world wide open for the advent of Big Business. The one merit of the book, according to Ford, is that such things as the helmet of Mambrino and the windmills are so badly depicted that we can still enjoy the beauty of the hero's character. Ford ends his criticism by dismissing *Don Quixote* as a work of propaganda, not of art.

JOHN GALSWORTHY (20th Century): Galsworthy, in answer to Ford Madox Ford's claim that Cervantes had ruined the chivalric spirit in Europe, claimed that Cervantes had one thing in common with all other writers, namely that he has not influenced humanity to any extent at all.

JOSEPH WOOD KRUTCH (20th Century): In *Five Masters,* Krutch claims that Cervantes was a Renaissance figure inasmuch as he inherited the best elements of that tradition. He goes on to say, however, that the importance of *Don Quixote* is that it breaks from the Renaissance tradition. There was in the 16th Century a revived interest in literature as an art form, which went hand in hand with a fresh examination of classical models. This led to the formation of certain set modes of literary expression, but it is important to note that *Don Quixote* belongs to none of them. There were two modes of expression clearly recognized, one of them aristocratic—as exemplified by the words of Homer and Virgil, for example, and the other plebeian and vulgar—as perfected by Boccaccio, for example. Literature was therefore on two levels, represented by the epic and the picareque. Cervantes' greatness was that he blended both with masterly skill, thus paving the way for a new era in the history of the novel.

ERNEST MERIMEE (20th Century): In *History of Spanish Literature,* he regards the various interpretations of the mysterious aspects of *Don Quixote* as being perfectly stupid. He is particularly contemptuous of the novel's being regarded in any way as a satire against the Church, politicians, Philip II and so on. He states most emphatically that Cervantes' novel has no hidden meaning whatsoever, or no esoteric riddles that have to be solved. He claims that it is quite simply an amusing, diverting tale of human failings, containing no elements of sadness whatsoever. It is merely the story by a man of wide experience and knowledge who is telling his readers that they should not trust their imaginations. Mérimée holds the opinion that the moral of the story is that men should accept life as it is and take men for what they are worth. Don Quixote, he tells, us, is not in any way a complicated character, but is a literary creation to be relished and enjoyed without searching for any deep meaning in his personality.

GEORGE TYLER NORTHRUP (20th Century): In *An Introduction to Spanish Literature,* Northrup says that Don Quixote is essentially a novel of humanity, exemplifying the democratic spirit of Spanish society. The philosophy it contains is of the homely kind, and is expressed mainly in the form of proverbs. He claims that Cervantes was by no means an original or revolutionary thinker. The author of *Don Quixote* was in many ways a conformist, accepting the religious, political, and literary opinions of the day. The critic caims that any rebellion on the part of Cervantes was from the heart rather than the mind. His thinking was imbued with Christian forgiveness, and contained no metaphysical subtleties whatsoever. Northrup concludes that *Don Quixote* is the world's greatest novel, not because of any greatness of technique, but because of the greatness of Cervantes' heart.

HERBERT READ (20th Century):   In *The Nature of Literature,* Read says that *Don Quixote,* far from mocking the human spirit, affirmed honor and chivalry. At the conclusion of a hard life, Cervantes had no illusions left. Nevertheless, he knew that glory as a sentiment was no illusion, and that only things done for the sake of glory were worth doing. Yet this is not the obvious interpretation of Cervantes, and although such phrases as "fair damsel in distress" and "the goodly Knight that pricketh on the plain" are very much in evidence, these are but part of a screen of mockery. If we penetrate this screen, we will find a great morality behind it.

GEORGE SANTAYANA (20th Century):   In his *Essays in Literary Criticism,* Santayana says that there is no suggestion in the book of premeditated satire, and that the author's obvious intention is to entertain, not to make accusations. His pathos does not contain any bitterness, because Cervantes had a healthy love for the world, and because at heart he was profoundly Christian. Santayana claims that Cervantes himself would have rejected any suggestion that his work was a critical commentary on religion and chivalry, since the author believed in these with profound conviction. If Cervantes were asked what the moral of *Don Quixote* was, he would probably have said that it was this: idealism is wasted on a force when the reality of life is not recognized. What made the chivalric ideal and Don Quixote's adventures so absurd was that the facts of daily life were neglected. Santayana says that idealism should not be surrendered, but that it should be made more powerful by a greater adjustment to reality.

MARK VAN DOREN (20th Century):   In a series of three essays collected under the heading *Don Quixote's Profession,* Van Doren expresses the point of view that a theory emerges from the book that the hero was, first and foremost, an actor. He was not only an actor, but he wrote his own play and kept himself on the center of the stage. As a matter of fact, he tells Sancho that plays are "the resemblance of realities" and should be loved because "they are all instrumental to the good of the commonwealth, and set before our eyes those looking-glasses that reflect a lively representation of human life; nothing being able to give us a more just idea of nature, and what we are or ought to be, than comedians and comedies." Mark Van Doren then poses the question of whether Don Quixote in fact confused man with actor or pretense with reality. He then claims that in the case of the knight, it is not impossible to assert that he always knows what he is doing, and that he has his own reasons for so doing. Dr. Van Doren ends this part of his statement by saying that Don Quixote is a completely created literary character, and is so real that we cannot be certain that we understand him.

SUBJECT BIBLIOGRAPHY

There have been many translations of *Don Quixote*, including one by Thomas Skelton in 1612, and one by the famous novelist, Tobias Smollett (the biography of Cervantes in this translation, incidentally, is worth examining). The best of the most recent translations, however, are those of Walter Starkie, Samuel Putnam, and J. M. Cohen. The Cohen translation, produced by Penguin Classics, is highly recommended for its fidelity to the spirit of the original text.

For a general survey of Cervantes and his works, the student should read Aubrey F. G. Bell's *Cervantes,* which covers such topics as Cervantes and the Renaissance, Cervantes' relationship to humor, reality, and the epic, etc. Gerald Brenan's *The Literature of the Spanish People* contains an excellent chapter on Cervantes (Chapter VIII), comprehensive in scope and penetrating in analytical insight.

In *Strains of Discord* by Robert M. Adams, there is a fascinating essay entitled "Two Lines from Cervantes," which expands some central themes of *Don Quixote* and places them in relation to the works of such writers as Flaubert and Stendhal. One of the most famous essays written on the hero of Cervantes' novel is Turgenev's "Hamlet and Don Quixote," which can be found in *Essays of the Masters,* edited by Charles Neider. It presents an interesting viewpoint which can be used as a point of departure to wider comparisons. One of the most readable yet incisively analytic works on *Don Quixote* is Mark Van Doren's *Don Quixote's Profession,* which is in fact the three *Walter Turner Candler Lectures* for 1956-57 delivered at Emory University. Dr. Van Doren presents some unique and provocative viewpoints which are well worth examining. An interesting book by Joseph Wood Krutch entitled *Five Masters* studies Cervantes' novel in juxtaposition to the works of Boccaccio, Richardson, Stendhal, and Proust. This is particularly interesting when read in conjunction with the Adams essay mentioned above. A short but beautifully developed essay on Cervantes is contained in

George Santayana's *Essays in Literary Criticism,* and this is highly recommended to students not only for its comprehensive survey of *Don Quixote,* but also for its own intrinsic merit as an essay of style and distinction.

On a more general level, J. Fitzmaurice-Kelly's *Chapters on Spanish Literature,* and G. T. Northrup's *An Introduction to Spanish Literature* could be read in conjunction for a general background in Spanish literary history. *A Handful of Authors,* by G. K. Chesterton, should certainly be read for interest, but with great caution as to the depths of its literary perception. For sheer amusement value only, the student is referred to the section on Cervantes in *The March of Literature,* by Ford Madox Ford. Ford's hysterical attack on Cervantes is almost brilliant in its absurdity. There are many histories of Spanish literature, of course, which contain brief but satisfactory chapters on Cervantes in general and Don Quixote in particular. Some of these are given in the general bibliography, together with a list of more specialized works on Cervantes which should give the student an above average background for a study of *Don Quixote.* Based on these works and the works mentioned above, topics for further study are then recommended. It should be remembered, however, that these are merely suggestions on which deeper studies can be based.

BIBLIOGRAPHY

GENERAL WORKS OF REFERENCE

Chapman, C. E., *A History of Spain*, 1918.
Fitzmaurice-Kelly, J., *Chapters on Spanish Literature*, 1908.
Fitzmaurice-Kelly, J., *The Relations Between Spanish and English Literature*, 1910.
Ford, J. D. M., *Main Currents of Spanish Literature*, 1919.
Hume, M. A. S., *Spanish Influence on English Literature*, 1905.
Hume, M. A. S., *Spain, Its Greatness and Decay*, 1898.
Hume, M. A. S., *The Spanish People, their Origin, Growth, and Influence*, 1901.
Merriman, R. B., *The Rise of the Spanish Empire in the Old World and the New*, 1918-25.
Peers, E. A., *Spain, a Companion to Spanish Studies*, 1929.

HISTORIES OF SPANISH LITERATURE

Adams, N. B., *The Heritage of Spain*, 1959.
Adams, N. B., and Keller, J. E., *Spanish Literature: A Brief Survey*, 1950.
Boggs, R., *Outline History of Spanish Literature*, 1939.
Brenan, G., *The Literature of the Spanish People*, 1957.
Clarke, H. B., *Spanish Literature, an Elementary Handbook*, 1893.
Fitzmaurice-Kelly, J., *A New History of Spanish Literature*, 1926.
Mérimée-Morley, *A History of Spanish Literature*, 1930.
Newmark, M., *Dictionary of Spanish Literature*, 1956.
Northrup, G. T., *An Introduction to Spanish Literature*, 1925.
Ticknor, G., *History of Spanish Literature*, 1888.

CERVANTES

Bates, M. J., *"Discrecion"* in *The Works of Cervantes*, 1945.
Buchanan, M. A., *The Works of Cervantes and Their Dates of Composition*, 1938.

Coleridge, S. T., *The Literary Remains,* Vol. I, pp. 113-131, 1836-39.

Duffield, A. J., *Don Quixote, His Critics and Commentators,* 1881.

Ellis, H., "Don Quixote" in *The Soul of Spain,* pp. 223-243, 1908.

Entwhistle, W. J., *Cervantes,* 1940.

Fitzmaurice-Kelly, J., *Cervantes and Shakespeare,* 1916.

Fitzmaurice-Kelly, J., *The Life of Miguel de Cervantes Saavedra,* 1892.

Fitzmaurice-Kelly, J., *Cervantes in England,* 1905.

Forster, J., "Lope de Vega and Cervantes" in *Some French and Spanish Men of Genius,* 1891.

Ker, W. J., *Two Essays on Don Quixote,* 1918.

Lowell, J. R., "Don Quixote" in *Democracy and Other Addresses,* 1887.

Prescott, W. H., "Sales *Don Quixote*", *North American Review,* Vol. XLV., 1837.

Raleigh, Sir W., *"Don Quixote"* in *Some Authors,* 1923.

Rennert, H. A., "Cervantes," in *University of Pennsylvania Lectures,* Vol. I., 1915.

Roscoe, T., *The Life and Writings of Miguel de Cervantes,* 1839.

Schevill, R., *Cervantes,* 1919.

Schevill, R., "Three Centuries of *Don Quixote,*" in *University of California Chronicle,* Vol. XV., 1913.

Smith, R., *The Life of Cervantes,* 1914.

Smollett, T., "Biography of Cervantes," in his translation of *Don Quixote,* 1755.

Thomas, Sir H., "Bibliographical Notes," in *Revue Hispanique,* Vol. XLV., 1919.

Watts, H. E., "Life of Cervantes," in *English Translation of Don Quixote,* Vol. I., 1888.

SUGGESTED TOPICS FOR FURTHER STUDY

1. Discuss the historical framework within which *Don Quixote* was written, with particular reference to is place in Renaissance literature.

2. To what extent does Cervantes succeed in blending the comic, tragic and allegorical elements in his story?

3. Some critics claim that there are great metaphysical dimensions to *Don Quixote*. Discuss the possibilities of their existence, with particular reference to the hero's relationship to the world around him.

4. What are the psychological and philosophical implications of the relationship between Don Quixote and Sancho Panza?

5. If social, religious, and political criticisms are implied in this book, how far does Cervantes succeed in concealing them behind the fabric of his narrative?

6. Discuss the way in which Cervantes unifies the picaresque and romantic traditions in his novel.

7. What symbolic role do the minor characters play in their relations with Don Quixote and Sancho Panza?

8. It has been suggested that Don Quixote is a religious figure, symbolizing Christian virtue. Would you say that this is a valid argument, and would you therefore describe the book as a religious allegory?

9. Discuss the interplay of fantasy and reality throughout the book.

10. Lord Byron said that Don Quixote "smil'd the chivalry of Spain away." Discuss this statement.

NOTES

NOTES

NOTES

NOTES

p 15,17,20,22,24-5
975